Knitting the Neighborhood

Knitting the Neighborhood

Official Knitting Patterns from
Mister Rogers' Neighborhood

sixth&springbooks

sixth&springbooks

An imprint of SOHO Publishing LLC
19 W 21st Street, Suite 601
New York, NY 10010
www.sixthandspring.com

Editor
JACOB SEIFERT

Art Director
IRENE LEDWITH

Patterns Editor
CARLA SCOTT

Contributing Patterns Editor
MELISSA DEHNCKE MCGILL

Technical Illustrator
LORETTA DACHMAN

Knitters
AUBREY BAUMGARTNER
JEANNIE CHIN
THERESE CHYNOWETH
MELISSA DEHNCKE MCGILL
DEBORAH T. O'NEILL

Photography
JACK DEUTSCH
WALT SENG: pages 11, 14, 27, 44,
    48, 62, 66, 73, 79, and 86
LILO GUEST: pages 19, 22, 52,
    and 56
RICHARD KELLY: pages 83, 95,
    and 98

Page Layout
DANITA ALBERT

Stylist
LINDSAY MORRIS

Hair and Makeup
CINDY ADAMS
LESLIE MAHAN

_____

Chief Executive Officer
CAROLINE KILMER

President
ART JOINNIDES

Chairman
JAY STEIN

WARNING: Buttons and other small items attached to knit items could present a choking
hazard. Take care to attach them securely. Supervise child at all times.

Library of Congress Cataloging-in-Publication Data
Names: Sixth & Spring Books, editor.
Title: Mister Rogers' neighborhood: knitting the neighborhood :
    official knitting patterns from Mister Rogers' neighborhood.
Description: First edition. | New York, New York : Sixth&Spring Books,
    2022. | Includes index.
Identifiers: LCCN 2022004920 | ISBN 9781970048100 (hardcover)
Subjects: LCSH: Knitting—Patterns. | Knitwear. | Mister Rogers'
    neighborhood (Television program)
Classification: LCC TT825 .M595 2022 | DDC 746.43/2041—dc23/eng/20220217
LC record available at https://lccn.loc.gov/2022004920

Manufactured in China

1 3 5 7 9 10 8 6 4 2

First Edition

Table of Contents

Introduction

Ask anyone who has ever watched *Mister Rogers' Neighborhood* what they remember about the show and they might mention the theme song, the trolley, or how Mister Rogers put on one of his cardigans at the beginning of every episode. If you ask a knitter, they're also likely to mention that nearly every one of Mister Rogers' sweaters was handknit.

Although it was not a theme focused upon, knitting was a constant throughout the series thanks to those ever-present cardigans. Lovingly stitched by his mother, Nancy Rogers, they were a perfect symbol for many of the messages that he taught: patience, perseverance, creativity, generosity. Furthermore, Mister Rogers encouraged us to slow down, to enjoy the moment, and to appreciate our own abilities, even if they aren't as developed as we would like them to be—all of which are attitudes that knitters should adopt while crafting.

Intended to celebrate the legacy of Mister Rogers, this first-ever collection of official knitting patterns from *Mister Rogers' Neighborhood* enables crafters to create cherished items from one of the most beloved television programs in American history. Even though he wore many different sweaters, most were similar or the same pattern knit in a variety of colors. Five of the most distinct cardigans to appear on the show were pulled from the screen and translated into knitting patterns, each with inclusive unisex sizing. For those who might not want zippers in their cardigans, guidance on how to alter the patterns to have buttons has been included. Additionally, one cardigan was sized for children, and two were adapted for babies (one as a cardigan and the other as an adorable onesie). Now, everyone in the family can have their own Mister Rogers cardigan.

Much more than just sweaters has been included in this collection. The entire world of *Mister Rogers' Neighborhood* can be viewed through the lens of knitting. You can knit accessories such as a necktie, Mr. McFeely's speedy delivery hat, or a scarf

inspired by the colorful curtains in Mister Rogers' living room. You can also stitch up four different puppets—King Friday, Queen Sara Saturday, X the Owl, and Daniel Striped Tiger—to populate your own Neighborhood of Make-Believe. Perhaps you'll want to create a miniature stoplight or even a little Mister Rogers himself, complete with interchangeable shoes and a tiny version of Daniel Striped Tiger. Three blankets, one whimsical baby blankie and two throws with Mister Rogers' words stitched in place, are also available for you to make and enjoy. With 24 patterns in all, there is plenty to knit for yourself and your loved ones.

You will also discover facts about and quotes from Mister Rogers, sure to leave you inspired and a little better acquainted with this entertainer, educator, father, and man. Charming photography from *Mister Rogers' Neighborhood* has also been sprinkled throughout.

As you work your way through your favorite patterns and learn more about Mister Rogers, we hope you are inspired to be a more patient and thoughtful crafter, are motivated to be a better neighbor to everyone you meet, and remember that it is always a beautiful day in the neighborhood when you're knitting. ■

Sweaters

Easy stitch patterns and Stockinette stitch combine with simple constructions in these replicas of Mister Rogers' cardigans. Helpful insight on finishing, including guidance on how to adapt patterns to have buttons rather zippers, can be found on pages 122–125.

Friendly Neighbor Cardigan

DESIGNED BY Carla Patrick

What is more iconic than Mister Rogers' bright red cardigan? Knit in simple and cozy Stockinette stitch, it will provide all the comfort and warmth you could want. This relaxed knitting experience will leave you with an easy-to-wear cardigan that will summon nostalgic memories of everyone's favorite neighbor.

FINISHED MEASUREMENTS

Chest 34½ (38, 40, 43, 46½, 50, 53, 56, 60)"/87.5 (96.5, 101.5, 109, 118, 127, 134.5, 142, 152.5)cm
Length 24½ (25, 25½, 26½, 27, 27½, 27½, 28½, 29)"/60 (62, 63.5, 64.5, 67.5, 68.5, 70, 72.5, 73.5)cm
Upper arm 11¼ (12, 13¼, 15½, 16, 17¼, 18, 18½, 19¼)"/ 28.5 (30.5, 33.5, 39.5, 40.5, 44, 46, 47, 49)cm

Shown in size with 43"/109cm chest.

MATERIALS

• 5 (5, 5, 6, 6, 7, 7, 8, 8) 3½oz/100g balls (each approx 218yd/196m) of Universal Yarn *Deluxe Worsted Superwash* (superwash wool) in 736 Christmas Red (4)
• One pair size 7 (4.5mm) needles, *or size to obtain gauge*
• Stitch markers
• One separating zipper 21 (22, 22, 24, 24, 24, 24, 25, 26)"/ 54 (56, 56, 61, 61, 61, 61, 64, 66)cm long in matching color
• Sewing needle and thread in matching color

GAUGE

20 sts and 28 rows to 4"/10cm over St st using size 7 (4.5mm) needles.
Take time to check gauge.

CARDIGAN
BACK

Cast on 87 (95, 101, 109, 117, 125, 133, 141, 151) sts.
Row 1 (RS) *K1, p1; rep from * to last st, k1.
Row 2 P1, *k1, p1; rep from * to end.
Rep last 2 rows for k1, p1 rib until piece measures 2"/5cm from beg, and dec 1 st at end of last WS row—86 (94, 100, 108, 116, 124, 132, 140, 150) sts.
Work even in St st (k on RS, p on WS) until piece measures 15½ (16, 16, 16, 16½, 16½, 16½, 17, 17)"/39.5 (40.5, 40.5, 40.2, 42, 42, 42, 53, 53)cm from beg, end with a WS row.

Armhole shaping

Cont in St st, bind off 5 (7, 8, 8, 9, 10, 10, 10, 11) sts at beg of next 2 rows, then 2 (3, 3, 4, 4, 5, 5, 6, 6) sts at beg of next 2 rows.
Dec row (RS) K2, k2tog, k to last 4 sts, ssk, k2—2 sts dec'd.
Next row Purl.
Rep last 2 rows 5 (5, 5, 6, 7, 7, 10, 11, 13) times more—60 (62, 66, 70, 74, 78, 80, 84, 88) sts.
Work even in St st until armhole measures 7½ (8, 8½, 9, 9½, 10, 10, 10½, 11)"/19 (20.5, 21.5, 23, 24, 25.5, 25.5, 26.5, 28)cm.

Shoulder and neck shaping

Note Shoulder and neck shaping are worked at the same time. Shoulder shaping is written out first, then neck shaping. Keep careful track of decreases.
Mark center 24 (24, 26, 28, 30, 30, 32, 34, 36) sts.
Cont in St st, bind off 4 (4, 4, 4, 5, 5, 5, 5, 6) sts at beg of next 8 (6, 4, 2, 8, 4, 4, 2, 8) rows, then 0 (5, 5, 5, 0, 6, 6, 6, 0) sts at beg of next 0 (2, 4, 6, 0, 4, 4, 6, 0) rows, AT THE SAME TIME, on first row of shoulder shaping, bind off center 24 (24, 26, 28, 30, 30, 32, 34, 36) sts and working both sides at once with separate balls of yarn, bind off 1 st from each neck edge twice.

LEFT FRONT

Cast on 44 (48, 50, 54, 58, 62, 66, 70, 74) sts.
Row 1 (RS) *K1, p1; rep from * to last 2 sts, k2.
Row 2 Sl 1, p1, *k1, p1; rep from * to end.
Rep last 2 rows for k1, p1 rib until piece measures 2"/5cm from beg, end with a WS row.
Next row (RS) Knit.
Next row Sl 1, p to end.
Rep last 2 rows for St st until same length as Back to armhole shaping, end with a WS row.

Armhole shaping

Dec row 1 (RS) Bind off 5 (7, 8, 8, 9, 10, 10, 10, 11) sts, k to end.
Row 2 Sl 1, p to end.
Dec row 3 Bind off 2 (3, 3, 4, 4, 5, 5, 6, 6) sts, k to end.

Mister Rogers experienced red-green color blindness, the most common form of color blindness. One day, he asked a co-worker to taste the soup he brought for lunch and tell him if it was pea or tomato soup. When asked why, he responded that if it were tomato soup he would add sugar to it.

Row 4 sl 1, p to end.
Dec row 5 K2, k2tog, k to end—1 st dec'd.
Row 6 Sl 1, p to end.
Rep last 2 rows 5 (5, 5, 6, 7, 7, 10, 11, 13) times more—31 (32, 33, 35, 37, 39, 40, 42, 43) sts.
Work even until armhole measures 5½ (6, 6½, 7, 7½, 8, 8, 8½, 9)"/(14, 15, 16.5, 18, 19, 20.5, 20.5, 21.5, 23)cm, end with a RS row.

Neck and shoulder shaping

Note Neck and shoulder shaping are worked at the same time. Neck shaping is written out first, then shoulder shaping begins when same length as Back to shoulder. Keep careful track of decreases.
Next row (WS) Bind off 5 (5, 5, 6, 7, 7, 8, 9, 9) sts (neck edge), p to end.
Dec row 1 (RS) K to last 3 sts, k2tog, k1—1 st dec'd.
Next row Purl.
Rep last 2 rows 4 times more.
Next row Rep dec row 1.
Dec row 2 (WS) P1, p2tog, p to end—1 st dec'd.
Rep last 2 rows once more, then rep dec row 1 once more, AT THE SAME TIME, when same length as Back to shoulder, bind off sts from shoulder edge (beg of RS rows) as foll: bind off 4 (4, 4, 4, 5, 5, 5, 5, 6) sts at beg of next 4 (3, 2, 1, 4, 2, 2, 1, 4) RS rows, then 0 (5, 5, 5, 0, 6, 6, 6, 0) sts at beg of next 0 (1, 2, 3, 0, 2, 2, 3, 0) RS rows.

RIGHT FRONT

Cast on 44 (48, 50, 54, 58, 62, 66, 70, 74) sts.

Row 1 (RS) K2, *p1, k1; rep from * to end.
Row 2 *P1, k1; rep from * to last 2 sts, p1, sl 1.
Rep last 2 rows for k1, p1 rib until piece measures 2"/5cm from beg, end with a WS row.
Next row (RS) Knit.
Next row P to last st, sl 1.
Rep last 2 rows for St st until same length as Back to armhole shaping, end with a RS row.

Armhole shaping

Row 1 (WS) Bind off 5 (7, 8, 8, 9, 10, 10, 10, 11) sts, p to last st, sl 1.
Row 2 Knit.
Dec row 3 Bind off 2 (3, 3, 4, 4, 5, 5, 6, 6) sts, p to last st, sl 1.
Row 4 Knit.
Row 5 P to last st, sl 1.
Dec row 6 (RS) K1, ssk, k to end.
Rep last 2 rows 5 (5, 5, 6, 7, 7, 10, 11, 13) times more—31 (32, 33, 35, 37, 39, 40, 42, 43) sts.
Work even until armhole measures 5½ (6, 6½, 7, 7½, 8, 8, 8½, 9)"/(14, 15, 16.5, 18, 19, 20.5, 20.5, 21.5, 23)cm, end with a WS row.

Neck and shoulder shaping

Note Neck and shoulder shaping are worked at the same time. Neck shaping is written out first, then shoulder shaping begins when same length as Back to shoulder. Keep careful track of decreases.
Next row (RS) Bind off 5 (5, 5, 6, 7, 7, 8, 9, 9) sts (neck edge), k to end.

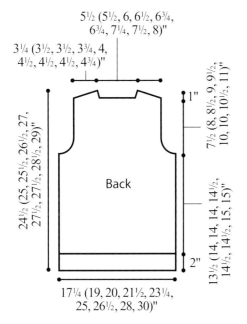
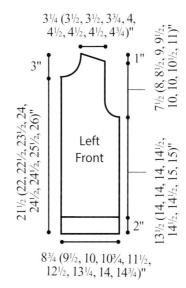
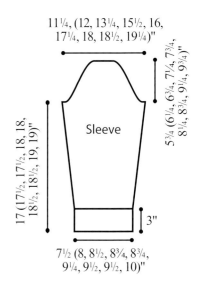

Next row Purl.
Dec row 1 (RS) K1, ssk, k to end.
Next row Purl
Rep last 2 rows 4 times more.
Next row Rep dec row 1.
Dec row 2 (WS) P to last 3 sts, p2tog, p1.
Rep last 2 rows once more, then rep dec row 1 once more, AT THE SAME TIME, when same length as Back to shoulder, bind off sts from shoulder edge (beg of WS rows) as foll: bind off 4 (4, 4, 4, 5, 5, 5, 5, 6) sts at beg of next 4 (3, 2, 1, 4, 2, 2, 1, 4) WS rows, then 0 (5, 5, 5, 0, 6, 6, 6, 0) sts at beg of next 0 (1, 2, 3, 0, 2, 2, 3, 0) WS rows. Bind off rem st.

SLEEVES

Cast on 39 (41, 43, 45, 45, 47, 49, 49, 51) sts.
Row 1 (RS) *K1, p1; rep from * to last st, k1.
Row 2 P1, *k1, p1; rep from * to end.
Rep last 2 rows for k1, p1 rib until piece measures 3"/7.5cm and dec 1 st on last WS row—38 (40, 42, 44, 44, 46, 48, 48, 50) sts.
Work in St st, inc 1 st each side every 10th (8th, 8th, 4th, 4th, 4th, 4th, 4th, 4th) row 9 (3, 12, 3, 6, 10, 13, 14, 17) times, then every 0 (10th, 0, 6th, 6th, 6th, 6th, 6th, 6th) row 0 (7, 0, 14, 12, 10, 8, 8, 6) times—56 (60, 66, 78, 80, 86, 90, 92, 96) sts.
Work even in St st until piece measures 17 (17½, 17½, 18, 18, 18½, 18½, 19, 19)"/43 (44.5, 44.5, 45.5, 45.5, 47, 47, 48, 48)cm from beg, end with a WS row.

Cap shaping

Cont in St st, bind off 5 (7, 8, 8, 9, 10, 10, 10, 11) sts at beg of next 2 rows, then 3 (3, 3, 4, 4, 5, 5, 6, 6) sts at beg of next 2 rows.
Work dec row as on Back armhole every 4th row 5 (3, 7, 7, 9, 10, 10, 11, 12) times, then every 6th (6th, 6th, 2nd, 2nd, 2nd, 2nd, 2nd, 2nd) row 2 (4, 2, 7, 5, 5, 7, 6, 6) times.
Bind off 3 sts at beg of next 4 rows.
Bind off rem 14 sts.

FINISHING

Weave in ends. Block pieces to measurements.
Sew shoulder seams. Set in sleeves. Sew side and sleeve seams.

Collar

Cast on 61 (61, 65, 69, 73, 73, 77, 81, 85) sts. Work in k1, p1 rib for 1 row.
Cast on 2 sts at beg of next 14 rows, working inc'd sts into rib—89 (89, 93, 97, 101, 101, 105, 109, 113) sts.
Work 2 rows even in rib.
Cont in rib, bind off 2 sts at beg of next 14 rows—61 (61, 65, 69, 73, 73, 77, 81, 85) sts. Work 1 row even, then bind off in rib. Fold collar in half with WS held tog. Sew in place around neck edge, sewing through both thicknesses.

Sew in zipper. ∎

Beginnings Cardigan

DESIGNED BY Carla Patrick

Streamlined details make this cardigan a delight to knit and wear.
Sleek Stockinette is worked for the fronts and backs while wide ribbing on
the sleeves lends itself nicely to the raglan shaping.

FINISHED MEASUREMENTS

Chest 34½ (38, 40, 43, 46½, 50, 53, 56, 60)"/87.5 (96.5,
101.5, 109, 118, 127, 134.5, 142, 152.5)cm
Length 26 (26½, 27, 28, 28½, 29, 29, 30, 30½)"/66 (67.5,
68.5, 71, 72.5, 73.5, 73.5, 76, 77.5)cm
Upper arm 11½ (12½, 13½, 15½, 16, 17½, 18, 18½,
19½)"/29 (32, 34, 39.5, 40.5, 44, 46, 47, 49.5)cm

Shown in size with 38"/96.5cm chest.

MATERIALS

• 6 (6, 7, 7, 8, 9, 9, 10, 10) 3½oz/100g skeins (each approx
210yd/193m) of Berroco *Comfort* (super fine acrylic/super fine
nylon) in 9782 Chianti 4
• One pair size 7 (4.5mm) needles, *or size to obtain gauge*
• One separating zipper 22 (22, 22, 24, 24, 24, 24, 26, 26)"/
56 (56, 56, 61, 61, 61, 61, 66, 66)cm long in matching color
• Sewing needle and thread in matching color
• Stitch markers
• Straight pins

GAUGE

20 sts and 28 rows to 4"/10cm over St st using size
7 (4.5mm) needles.
Take time to check gauge.

CENTER RIB PATTERN

(over 27 sts)
Row 1 (RS) [P3, k5] 3 times, p3.
Row 2 [K3, p5] 3 times, k3.
Rep rows 1 and 2 for center rib pat.

CARDIGAN
BACK

Cast on 86 (94, 102, 110, 118, 126, 134, 142, 150) sts.
Row 1 (RS) *K2, p2; rep from * to last 2 sts, k2.
Row 2 P2, *k2, p2; rep from * to end.
Rep last 2 rows for k2, p2 rib until piece measures 2"/5cm from
beg, and dec 0 (0, 2, 2, 2, 2, 2, 2, 0) sts on last WS row—86
(94, 100, 108, 116, 124, 132, 140, 150) sts.

Work even in St st (k on RS, p on WS) until piece measures 15½
(15½, 15½, 16, 16, 16, 16, 16½, 16½)"/39.5 (39.5, 39.5, 40.5,
40.5, 40.5, 40.5, 42, 42)cm from beg, end with a WS row.

Armhole shaping

Cont in St st, bind off 2 (2, 3, 4, 5, 7, 9, 9, 9) sts at beg of next
2 rows—82 (90, 94, 100, 106, 110, 114, 122, 132) sts.

For chest size 34½"/87.5cm only
Dec row (RS) K1, k2tog, k to last 3 sts, SKP, k1—2 sts dec'd.
Work 3 rows even in St st.
Rep last 4 rows twice more—76 sts.

*For chest sizes 46½ (50, 53, 56, 60)"/118 (127, 134.5,
142, 152.5)cm only*
Dec row (RS) K1, k3tog, k to last 4 sts, SK2P, k1—4 sts dec'd.
Next row Purl.
Rep last 2 rows 0 (0, 1, 2, 5) times more—102 (106, 106, 110,
108) sts.

For all sizes
Dec row (RS) K1, k2tog, k to last 3 sts, SKP, k1—2 sts dec'd.
Next row Purl.
Rep last 2 rows 27 (31, 33, 35, 35, 37, 36, 36, 36) times—20
(26, 26, 28, 30, 30, 32, 36, 34) sts.
Bind off rem sts for back neck.

LEFT FRONT

Cast on 46 (50, 50, 54, 58, 62, 66, 70, 78) sts.
Row 1 (RS) *K2, p2; rep from * to last 2 sts, k2.
Row 2 Sl 1, p1, *k2, p2; rep from * to end.
Rep last 2 rows for k2, p2 rib until piece measures 2"/5cm from
beg, and dec 2 (2, 0, 0, 0, 0, 0, 0, 2) sts on last WS row (do not
work dec over first 2 sts)—44 (48, 50, 54, 58, 62, 66, 70, 76) sts.
Next row (RS) Knit.
Next row Sl 1, p to end.
Rep last 2 rows for St st until same length as back to armhole
shaping, end with a WS row.

In total, nearly 900 episodes of *Mister Rogers' Neighborhood were produced. This beloved television show, like many other classics, first aired in black and white before it was broadcast in color.*

Beginnings Cardigan

Armhole and neck shaping

Dec row (RS) Bind off 2 (2, 3, 4, 5, 7, 9, 9, 9) sts, k to end—42 (46, 47, 50, 53, 55, 57, 61, 67) sts.
Next row Sl 1, p to end.

For chest size 34½"/87.5cm only
Dec row (RS) K1, k2tog, k to end—1 st dec'd.
Work 3 rows even in St st, with sl 1 at beg of WS rows.
Rep last 4 rows twice more—39 sts.

For chest sizes 46½ (50, 53, 56, 60)"/118 (127, 134.5, 142, 152.5)cm only
Dec row (RS) K1, k3tog, k to end—2 sts dec'd.
Next row Sl 1, p to end.
Rep last 2 rows 0 (0, 1, 2, 5) times more—51 (53, 53, 55, 55) sts.

For all sizes
Dec row (RS) K1, k2tog, k to end—1 st dec'd.
Next row Sl 1, p to end.
Rep last 2 rows until there are 21 (24, 23, 24, 26, 25, 26, 26, 28) sts, end with a RS row.
Next row (WS) Bind off 4 (5, 4, 5, 5, 5, 5, 7) sts, p to end.
Cont armhole dec at beg of RS rows, AT THE SAME TIME, dec 1 st at neck edge at end of every RS row 5 (5, 5, 5, 6, 6, 5, 5, 5) times, then every row 4 (4, 4, 4, 4, 6, 6, 6) times.

RIGHT FRONT
Cast on 46 (50, 50, 54, 58, 62, 68, 78) sts.
Row 1 (RS) K2, *p2, k2; rep from * to end.

Row 2 *P2, k2; rep from * to last 2 sts, p1, sl 1.
Rep last 2 rows for k2, p2 rib until piece measures 2"/5cm from beg, and dec 2 (2, 0, 0, 0, 0, 0, 2, 2) sts on last WS row (do not work dec over last 2 sts—44 (48, 50, 54, 58, 62, 66, 70, 76) sts.
Next row (RS) Knit.
Next row (WS) P to last st, sl 1.
Rep last 2 rows for St st until same length as Back to armhole shaping, end with a RS row.

Armhole and neck shaping
Next row (WS) Bind off 2 (2, 3, 4, 5, 7, 9, 9, 9) sts, p to last st, sl 1—42 (46, 47, 50, 53, 55, 57, 61, 67) sts.
Next row Knit.
Next row P to last st, sl 1.

For chest size 34½"/87.5cm only
Dec row (RS) K to last 3 sts, SKP, k1—1 st dec'd.
Work 3 rows even in St st, with sl 1 at end of WS rows.
Rep last 4 rows twice more—39 sts.

For chest sizes 46½ (50, 53, 56, 60)"/118 (127, 134.5, 142, 152.5)cm only
Dec row (RS) K to last 4 sts, SK2P, k1—2 sts dec'd.
Next row P to last st, sl 1.
Rep last 2 rows (0, 0, 1, 2, 5) times more—51 (53, 55, 55) sts.

For all sizes
Dec row (RS) K to last 3 sts, SKP, k1—1 st dec'd.
Next row P to last st, sl 1.

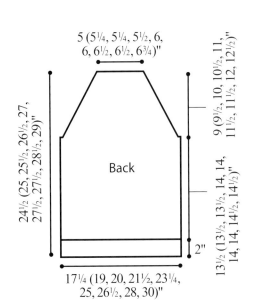

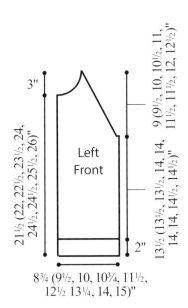

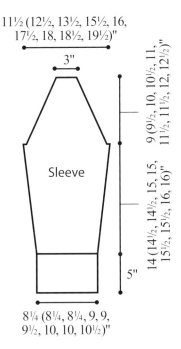

Rep last 2 rows until there are 21 (24, 23, 24, 26, 25, 26, 26, 28) sts, end with a WS row.
Next row (RS) Bind off 4 (5, 4, 5, 5, 5, 5, 7) sts, k to end.
Cont armhole dec at end of RS rows, AT THE SAME TIME, dec 1 st at neck edge at beg of every RS row 5 (5, 5, 5, 6, 6, 5, 5) times, then every row 4 (4, 4, 4, 4, 4, 6, 6, 6) times.

SLEEVES
Cast on 42 (42, 42, 46, 46, 46, 50, 50, 50) sts.
Row 1 (RS) *K2, p2; rep from * to last 2 sts, k2.
Row 2 P2, *k2, p2; rep from * to end.
Rep last 2 rows for k2, p2 rib until piece measures 5"/7.5cm, and inc 1 (1, 1, 1, 1, 3, 1, 1, 3) sts on last WS row—43 (43, 43, 47, 47, 49, 51, 51, 53) sts.

Center rib pattern
Next row (RS) Work in St st over 8 (8, 8, 10, 10, 11, 12, 12, 13) sts, pm, work row 1 of center rib pat over 27 sts, work in St st over 8 (8, 8, 10, 10, 11, 12, 12, 13) sts.
Cont in pats as established and inc 1 st each side (working inc sts into St st) every 10th (8th, 6th, 6th, 4th, 4th, 4th, 4th, 4th) row 3 (3, 5, 16, 6, 10, 13, 14, 17) times, then every 12th (10th, 8th, 0, 6th, 6th, 6th, 6th, 6th) row 5 (7, 8, 0, 12, 10, 8, 8, 6) times—59 (63, 69, 79, 83, 89, 93, 95, 99) sts.
Work even in pat until piece measures 14 (14½, 14½, 15, 15, 15½, 15½, 16, 16)"/35.5 (37, 37, 38, 38, 39.5, 39.5, 40.5, 40.5)cm above rib, end with a WS row.

Raglan cap shaping
Cont in St st, bind off 2 (2, 3, 4, 5, 7, 9, 9, 9) sts at beg of next 2 rows.
Dec row (RS) K1, k2tog, k to last 3 sts, SKP, k1—2 sts dec'd.
Next row Purl.
Rep last 2 rows 8 (11, 13, 19, 20, 20, 20, 20, 22) times more.
Rep dec row.
Work 3 rows even.
Rep last 4 rows 10 (9, 9, 7, 8, 8, 8, 9, 9) times more.
Bind off rem 15 sts.

FINISHING
Weave in ends. Block pieces to measurements.
Sew raglan sleeve caps into raglan armholes.
Sew side and sleeve seams.

Collar
Cast on 62 (62, 62, 62, 66, 66, 66, 66, 70) sts. Work in k2, p2 rib for 1 row.

*"**Often when you think you're at the end of something, you're at the beginning of something else.**"*

Cast on 2 sts at beg of next 14 rows, working inc sts into rib—90 (90, 90, 90, 94, 94, 94, 94, 98) sts.
Work 2 rows even in rib.
Cont in rib, bind off 2 sts at beg of next 14 rows—62 (62, 62, 62, 66, 66, 66, 66, 70) sts.
Work 1 row even, then bind off in rib.
Fold collar in half with WS held tog. Sew in place around neck edge, sewing through both thicknesses.

Sew in zipper. ■

Generosity Cardigan

DESIGNED BY Carla Patrick

With the body worked in reverse Stockinette stitch, this cardigan brought
an entirely different look to Mister Rogers' wardrobe. Ribbing is picked up along
the fronts and neck and then finished off with a tidy black trim detail.

FINISHED MEASUREMENTS
Chest 35 (38, 40, 43, 46½, 50, 53, 56, 60)"/87.5 (96.5, 101.5, 109, 118, 127, 134.5,142, 152.5)cm
Length 24 (25, 25½, 26½, 27, 27½, 27½, 28½, 29)"/61 (63.5, 64.5, 67.5, 68.5, 70, 70, 72, 73.5)cm
Upper arm 11¼ (12, 13¼, 15½, 16, 17¼, 18, 18½, 19¼)"/ 28.5 (30.5, 33.5, 39.5, 40.5, 44, 46, 47, 49)cm

Shown in size with 43"/109cm chest.

MATERIALS
• 5 (5, 6, 6, 7, 7, 8, 8, 9) 3½oz/100g skeins (each approx 177m/194yd) of Patons *Classic Wool Worsted* (wool) in Heath Heather (MC) (4)
• 1 skein in Black (CC)
• One pair size 7 (4.5mm) needles, *or size to obtain gauge*
• One size 7 (4.5mm) circular needle, 24"/58cm long
• One black separating zipper 21 (22, 22, 24, 24, 24, 24, 25, 26)"/54 (56, 56, 61, 61, 61, 61, 64, 66)cm long
• Sewing needle and thread in matching color
• Stitch markers

GAUGE
20 sts and 28 rows to 4"/10cm over rev St st using size 7 (4.5mm) needles.
Take time to check gauge.

CARDIGAN
BACK
With CC, cast on 87 (95, 101, 109, 117, 125, 133, 141, 151) sts.
Row 1 (RS) *K1, p1; rep from * to last st, k1.
Row 2 P1, *k1, p1; rep from * to end.
Cut CC. Join MC and knit 1 row on RS.
Work row 2 once more, then rep rows 1 and 2 for k1, p1 rib until piece measures 2"/5cm from beg, and dec 1 st at end of last WS row—86 (94, 100, 108, 116, 124, 132, 140, 150) sts.
Work even in rev St st (p on RS, k on WS) until piece measures 15½ (16, 16, 16½, 16½, 16½, 16½, 17, 17)"/39.5 (40.5, 40.5, 42, 42, 42, 42, 43, 43)cm from beg, end with a WS row.

Armhole shaping
Cont in rev St st, bind off 5 (7, 8, 8, 9, 10, 10, 10, 11) sts at beg of next 2 rows, then 2 (3, 3, 4, 4, 5, 5, 6, 6) sts at beg of next 2 rows.
Dec row (RS) P2, p2tog, p to last 4 sts, p2tog, p2—2 sts dec'd.
Next row Knit.
Rep last 2 rows 5 (5, 5, 6, 7, 7, 10, 11, 13) times more—60 (62, 66, 70, 74, 78, 80, 84, 88) sts.
Work even in rev St st until armhole measures 7½ (8, 8½, 9, 9½, 10, 10, 10½, 11)"/19 (20.5, 21.5, 23, 24, 25.5, 25.5, 26.5, 28)cm.

Shoulder and neck shaping
Note Shoulder and neck shaping are worked at the same time. Shoulder shaping is written out first, then neck shaping. Keep careful track of decreases.
Mark center 24 (24, 26, 28, 30, 30, 32, 34, 36) sts.
Bind off 4 (4, 4, 4, 5, 5, 5, 5, 6) at beg of next 8 (6, 4, 2, 8, 4, 4, 2, 8) rows, 0 (5, 5, 5, 0, 6, 6, 6, 0) sts at beg of next 0 (2, 4, 6, 0, 4, 4, 6, 0) rows, AT THE SAME TIME, on the first row of shoulder shaping, bind off center 24 (24, 26, 28, 30, 30, 32, 34, 36) sts and working both sides at once with separate balls of yarn, bind off 1 st from each neck edge twice.

LEFT FRONT
With CC, cast on 39 (43, 45, 49, 53, 57, 61, 65, 69) 49 sts and work as for Back until piece measures 2"/5cm from beg, and dec

Many of the sweaters Mister Rogers wore on Mister Rogers' Neighborhood were hand knit for him by his mother, Nancy Rogers. She would knit him a new sweater every year and give it to him as a Christmas present. A prolific and generous knitter, she also knit sweaters for others throughout the year, averaging one sweater a month.

1 st on last WS row—38 (42, 44, 48, 52, 56, 60, 64, 68) sts. Work even in rev St st until same length as Back to armhole shaping, end with a WS row.

Armhole shaping

Dec row 1 (RS) Bind off 5 (7, 8, 8, 9, 10, 10, 10, 11) sts, p to end.
Row 2 Knit.
Dec row 3 Bind off 2 (3, 3, 4, 4, 5, 5, 6, 6) sts, p to end.
Row 4 Knit.
Dec row 5 P2, p2tog, p to end—1 st dec'd.
Row 6 Knit.
Rep last 2 rows 5 (5, 5, 6, 7, 7, 10, 11, 13) times more—25 (26, 27, 29, 31, 33, 34, 36, 37) sts.
Work even in rev St st until armhole measures 5½ (6, 6½, 7, 7½, 8, 8, 8½, 9)"/(14, 15, 16.5, 18, 19, 20.5, 20.5, 21.5, 23)cm, end with a RS row

Neck and shoulder shaping

Note Neck and shoulder shaping are worked at the same time. Neck shaping is written out first, then shoulder shaping begins when same length as Back to shoulder. Keep careful track of decreases.
Next row (WS) Bind off 3 (3, 3, 4, 5, 5, 6, 7, 7) sts (neck edge), k to end.
Dec row 1 P to last 3 sts, p2tog, p1.
Next row Knit.
Rep last 2 rows 5 times more, AT THE SAME TIME, when same length as Back to shoulder, bind off sts from shoulder edge (beg of RS rows) as foll: 4 (4, 4, 4, 5, 5, 5, 5, 6) sts at beg of next 4 (3, 2, 1, 4, 2, 2, 1, 4) RS rows, and then 0 (5, 5, 5, 0, 6, 6, 6, 0) sts at beg of next 0 (1, 2, 3, 0, 2, 2, 3, 0) RS rows.

RIGHT FRONT

With CC, cast on 39 (43, 45, 49, 53, 57, 61, 65, 69) 49 sts and work as for Back until piece measures 2"/5cm from beg, and dec 1 st on last WS row—38 (42, 44, 48, 52, 56, 60, 64, 68) sts. Work even in rev St st until same length as Back to armhole shaping, end with a RS row.

Armhole shaping

Dec row 1 (WS) Bind off 5 (7, 8, 8, 9, 10, 10, 10, 11) sts, k to end.
Row 2 Purl.
Dec row 3 Bind off 2 (3, 3, 4, 4, 5, 5, 6, 6) sts, k to end.
Row 4 Purl.
Dec row 5 K2, k2tog, k to end—1 st dec'd.
Row 6 Purl.
Rep last 2 rows 5 (5, 5, 6, 7, 7, 10, 11, 13) times more—25 (26, 27, 29, 31, 33, 34, 36, 37) sts.
Work even in rev St st until armhole measures 5½ (6, 6½, 7, 7½, 8, 8, 8½, 9)"/(14, 15, 16.5, 18, 19, 20.5, 20.5, 21.5, 23)cm, end with a WS row.

Neck and shoulder shaping

Note Neck and shoulder shaping are worked at the same time. Neck shaping is written out first, then shoulder shaping begins when same length as Back to shoulder. Keep careful track of decreases.
Next row (RS) Bind off 3 (3, 3, 4, 5, 5, 6, 7, 7) sts (neck edge), p to end.
Next row Knit.
Dec row 1 (RS) P1, p2tog, p to end.
Next row Knit.
Rep last 2 rows 5 times more, AT THE SAME TIME, when same

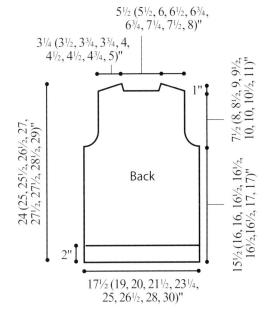

5½ (5½, 6, 6½, 6¾, 6¾, 7¼, 7½, 8)"
3¼ (3½, 3¾, 3¾, 4, 4½, 4½, 4¾, 5)"
1"
7½ (8, 8½, 9, 9½, 10, 10, 10½, 11)"
24 (25, 25½, 26½, 27, 27½, 27½, 28½, 29)"
Back
15½ (16, 16, 16½, 16½, 16½, 16½, 17, 17)"
2"
17½ (19, 20, 21½, 23¼, 25, 26½, 28, 30)"
3¼ (3½, 3¾, 3¾, 4, 4½, 4½, 4¾, 5)"
3"
1"
7½ (8, 8½, 9, 9½, 10, 10, 10½, 11)"
21 (22, 22½, 23½, 24, 24½, 24½, 25½, 26)"
Left Front
15½ (16, 16, 16½, 16½, 16½, 16½, 17, 17)"
7¾ (8½, 9, 9½, 10½, 11¼, 12, 13, 13½)"
11¼ (12, 13¼, 15½, 16, 17¼, 18, 18½, 19¼)"
5¾ (6¼, 6¾, 7¼, 7¾, 8¼, 8¾, 9¼, 9¾)"
17 (17½, 17½, 18, 18, 18½, 18½, 19, 19)"
Sleeve
3"
7½ (8, 8½, 8¾, 8¾, 9¼, 9½, 9½, 10)"

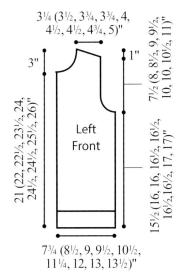

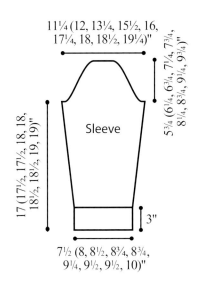

length as Back to shoulder, bind off sts from shoulder edge (beg of WS rows) as foll: 4 (4, 4, 4, 5, 5, 5, 5, 6) sts at beg of next 4 (3, 2, 1, 4, 2, 2, 1, 4) WS rows, and then 0 (5, 5, 5, 0, 6, 6, 6, 0) sts at beg of next 0 (1, 2, 3, 0, 2, 2, 3, 0) WS rows.

SLEEVES

With CC, cast on 39 (41, 43, 45, 45, 47, 49, 49, 51) sts and work rib as for Back until rib measures 3"/7.5cm, dec 1 st on last WS row—38 (40, 42, 44, 44, 46, 48, 48, 50) sts.
Work in rev St st, inc 1 st each side every 10th (8th, 8th, 4th, 4th, 4th, 4th, 4th, 4th) row 9 (3, 12, 3, 6, 10, 13, 14, 17) times, then every 0 (10th, 0, 6th, 6th, 6th, 6th, 6th, 6th) row 0 (7, 0, 14, 12, 10, 8, 8, 6) times—56 (60, 66, 78, 80, 86, 90, 92, 96) sts.
Work even in rev St st until piece measures 17 (17½, 17½, 18, 18, 18½, 18½, 19, 19)"/43 (44.5, 44.5, 45.5, 45.5, 48, 48)cm from beg, end with a WS row.

Cap shaping

Cont in rev St st, bind off 5 (7, 8, 8, 9, 10, 10, 10, 11) sts at beg of next 2 rows, 3 (3, 3, 4, 4, 5, 5, 6, 6) sts at beg of next 2 rows.
Work dec row as on Back armhole every 4th row 5 (3, 7, 7, 11, 10, 10, 11, 12) times, then every 6th (6th, 6th, 2nd, 2nd, 2nd, 2nd, 2nd, 2nd) row 2 (4, 2, 7, 5, 5, 7, 6, 6) times.
Bind off 3 sts at beg of next 4 rows.
Bind off rem 14 sts.

FINISHING

Weave in ends. Block pieces to measurements.
Sew shoulder seams. Set in sleeves. Sew side and sleeve seams.

Right front band and half collar

With RS facing, circular needle and MC, beg at lower edge of Right Front, pick up and k 117 (123, 124, 130, 132, 136, 136, 140, 145) sts along Right Front edge to beg of neck shaping, pm, pick up and k 15 (15, 15, 16, 17, 17, 18, 19, 19) sts along Right Front neck, and pick up and k 15 (15, 16, 17, 18, 18, 19, 20, 21) sts along half of Back neck—147 (153, 155, 163, 167, 171, 173, 179, 185) sts.
Row 1 (WS) P1, *k1, p1; rep from * to end.
This row has established your rib. Maintain rib in foll rows and work inc's into rib.
Inc row 2 Work in rib to marker, M1 if last st was a purl st or M1-p if last st was a knit st, sm, work 1 st, M1 if next st is a purl st or M1-p if next st is a knit st, work in rib to end—2 sts inc'd.
Row 3 K the knit sts and p the purl sts.
Rep last 2 rows twice more. Cut MC. Join CC
Knit 1 row on RS. Knit 1 row more, then bind off all sts loosely.

Left front band and half collar

With RS facing, circular needle and MC, beg at center back neck, pick up and k 15 (15, 16, 17, 18, 18, 19, 20, 21) sts along 2nd

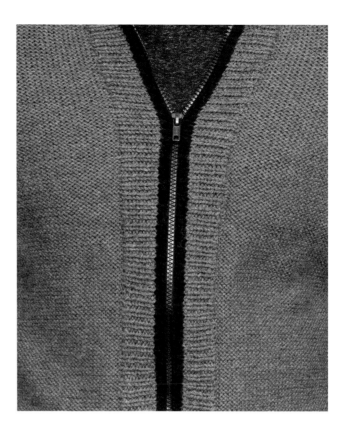

half of Back neck, pick up and k 15 (15, 15, 16, 17, 17, 18, 19, 19) sts along Left Front neck, pm, and pick up and k 117 (123, 124, 130, 132, 136, 136, 140, 145) sts along Left Front to lower edge—147 (153, 155, 163, 167, 171, 173, 179, 185) sts.
Row 1 (WS) P1, *k1, p1; rep from * to end.
This row has established your rib. Maintain rib in foll rows and work inc's into rib.
Inc row 2 Work in rib to marker, M1 if last st was a purl st or M1-p if last st was a knit st, sm, work 1 st, M1 if next st is a purl st or M1-p if next st is a knit st, work in rib to end—2 sts inc'd.
Row 3 K the knit sts and p the purl sts.
Rep last 2 rows twice more.
Cut MC. Join CC and knit 1 row on RS. Knit 1 row more, then bind off all sts loosely.

Sew sides of collar tog at center back neck.
Sew in zipper. ∎

"... each one of us has something valuable to bring to this world. That's one of the things that connects us as neighbors—in our own way, each one of us is a giver and a receiver."

Nurture Cardigan

DESIGNED BY Carla Patrick

Four cables, each cozy in its own narrow bed of reverse Stockinette stitch, add surface texture to the classic Mister Rogers cardigan. A simple ribbing ties in nicely as it climbs alongside the front cables and zipper to the ribbed collar.

◀━■■▭

FINISHED MEASUREMENTS

Chest 34½ (38, 40, 43, 46½, 50, 53, 56, 60)"/87.5 (96.5, 101.5, 109, 118, 127, 134.5, 142, 152.5)cm
Length 24 (25, 25½, 26, 27, 27½, 27½, 28½, 29)"/61 (63.5, 64.5, 66, 68.5, 70, 70, 72, 73.5)cm
Upper arm 11¼ (12, 13¼, 15½, 16, 17¼, 18, 18½, 19¼)"/ 28.5 (30.5, 33.5, 39.5, 40.5, 44, 46, 47, 49)cm

Shown in size with 38"/96.5cm chest.

MATERIALS

• 9 (10, 11, 12, 13, 14, 15, 16, 18) 1¾oz/50g skeins (each approx 109yd/100m) of Sandnes Garn *Alpakka Ull* (alpaca/wool) in 7755 Emerald (**4**)
• One pair size 7 (4.5mm) needles, *or size to obtain gauges*
• One separating zipper 21 (22, 22, 24, 24, 24, 24, 25, 26)"/ 54 (56, 58, 58, 61, 61, 61, 64, 66)cm long in matching color
• Sewing needle and thread in matching color
• Cable needle (cn)
• Stitch markers

GAUGES

• 20 sts and 28 rows to 4"/10cm over rev St st using size 7 (4.5mm) needles.
• 10 sts to 1½"/4cm over cable panel using size 7 (4.5mm) needles.
TAKE TIME TO CHECK GAUGES.

CABLE PANEL

(over 10 sts)
Rows 1 and 3 (RS) P2, k6, p2.
Row 2 and all WS rows K2, p6, k2.
Row 5 P2, 6-st LC, p2.
Row 7 P2, k6, p2.
Row 8 K2, p6, k2.
Rep rows 1–8 for cable panel.

STITCH GLOSSARY

6-st LC Sl 3 sts to cn and hold to front, k3, k3 from cn.

CARDIGAN

BACK

Cast on 87 (95, 101, 109, 117, 125, 133, 141, 151) sts.
Row 1 (RS) *K1, p1; rep from * to last st, k1.
Row 2 P1, *k1, p1; rep from * to end.
Rep last 2 rows for k1, p1 rib until piece measures 2"/5cm from beg, and dec 1 st at end of last WS row—86 (94, 100, 108, 116, 124, 132, 140, 150) sts.
Work even in St st (k on RS, p on WS) until piece measures 15½ (16, 16, 16, 16½, 16½, 16½, 17, 17)"/39.5 (40.5, 40.5, 40.5, 42, 42, 42, 43, 43)cm from beg, end with a WS row.

Armhole shaping

Cont in St st, bind off 5 (7, 8, 8, 9, 10, 10, 10, 11) sts at beg of next 2 rows, then 2 (3, 3, 4, 4, 5, 5, 6, 6) sts at beg of next 2 rows.
Dec row (RS) K2, k2tog, k to last 4 sts, ssk, k2.
Next row Purl.
Rep last 2 rows 5 (5, 5, 6, 7, 7, 10, 11, 13) times more—60, (62, 66, 70, 74, 78, 80, 84, 88) sts.
Work even in St st until armhole measures 7½ (8, 8½, 9, 9½, 10, 10, 10½, 11)"/19 (20.5, 21.5, 23, 24, 25.5, 25.5, 26.5, 28)cm.

Shoulder and neck shaping

Note Shoulder and neck shaping are worked at the same time. Shoulder shaping is written out first, then neck shaping. Keep careful track of decreases.
Mark center 24 (24, 26, 28, 30, 30, 32, 34, 36) sts.
Bind off 4 (4, 4, 4, 5, 5, 5, 5, 6) sts at beg of next 8 (6, 4, 2, 8, 4, 4, 2, 8) rows, 0 (5, 5, 5, 0, 6, 6, 6, 0) sts at beg of next 0 (2, 4, 6, 0, 4, 4, 6, 0) rows, AT THE SAME TIME, on first row of shoulder shaping bind off center 24 (24, 26, 28, 30, 30, 32, 34, 36) sts, and working both sides at once with separate balls of yarn, bind off 1 st from each neck edge twice.

LEFT FRONT

Cast on 46 (50, 52, 56, 60, 64, 68, 72, 76) sts.
Row 1 (RS) *K1, p1; rep from * to last 2 sts, k2.
Row 2 Sl 1, p1, *k1, p1; rep from * to end.
Rep last 2 rows for k1, p1 rib until piece measures 2"/5cm from

Mister Rogers originally thought children's television to be "perfectly horrible" and desired to harness its power to nurture young people. Many years later, a study from Yale University found that children retained more from watching Mister Rogers' Neighborhood than they did from watching Sesame Street.

beg, and inc 1 st at end of last WS row—47 (51, 53, 57, 61, 65, 69, 73, 77) sts.

Begin patterns

Row 1 (RS) K to last 16 sts for St st, pm, work row 1 of cable panel over 10 sts, pm, [k1, p1] twice, k2 for rib.
Row 2 Sl 1, p1, [k1, p1] twice for rib, sm, work row 2 of cable panel over 10 sts, sm, p to end for St st.
Work even in pats as established until same length as Back to armhole shaping, end with a WS row.

Armhole shaping

Dec row 1 (RS) Bind off 5 (7, 8, 8, 9, 10, 10, 10, 11) sts, cont in pats to end.
Row 2 Work even in pats.
Dec row 3 Bind off 2 (3, 3, 4, 4, 5, 5, 6, 6) sts, cont in pats to end.
Row 4 Work even in pats.
Dec row 5 K2, k2tog, cont in pats to end—1 st dec'd.
Row 6 Work even in pats.
Rep last 2 rows 5 (5, 5, 6, 7, 7, 10, 11, 13) times more—34 (35, 36, 38, 40, 42, 43, 45, 46) sts.
Work even in pats until armhole measures 5½ (6, 6½, 7, 7½, 8, 8, 8½, 9)"/14 (15.5, 16.5, 18, 19, 20.5, 20.5, 21.5, 23)cm, end with a RS row.

Neck and Shoulder Shaping

Note Neck and shoulder shaping are worked at the same time. Neck shaping is written out first, then shoulder shaping begins when same length as Back to shoulder. Keep careful track of decreases.
Next row (WS) Bind off 8 (8, 8, 9, 10, 10, 11, 12, 12) sts (neck edge), cont in pats to end.

Dec row 1 (RS) Work to last 3 sts, k2tog, k1—1 st dec'd.
Next row Work even in pats.
Rep last 2 rows 4 times more.
Next row Rep dec row 1.
Dec row 2 (WS) P1, p2tog, work to end—1 st dec'd.
Rep last 2 rows once more, then rep dec row 1 once more, AT THE SAME TIME, when same length as Back to shoulder, bind off sts from shoulder edge (beg of RS rows) as foll: bind off 4 (4, 4, 4, 5, 5, 5, 5, 6) sts at beg of next 4 (3, 2, 1, 4, 2, 1, 4) RS rows, then 0 (5, 5, 5, 0, 6, 6, 6, 0) sts at beg of next 0 (1, 2, 3, 0, 2, 2, 3, 0) RS rows.

RIGHT FRONT

Cast on 46 (50, 52, 56, 60, 64, 68, 72, 76) sts.
Row 1 (RS) K2, *p1, k1; rep from * to end.
Row 2 *P1, k1; rep from * to last 2 sts, p1, sl 1.
Rep last 2 rows for k1, p1 rib until piece measures 2"/5cm from beg, and inc 1 st at beg of last WS row—47 (51, 53, 57, 61, 65, 69, 73, 77) sts.

Begin patterns

Row 1 (RS) K2, [p1, k1] twice for rib, pm, work row 1 of cable panel over 10 sts, pm, k to end for St st.
Row 2 P to last 16 sts for St st, sm, work row 2 of cable panel over 10 sts, sm, [p1, k1] twice, p1, sl 1 for rib.
Work even in pats as established until same length as Back to armhole shaping, end with a RS row.

Armhole shaping

Dec row 1 (WS) Bind off 5 (7, 8, 8, 9, 10, 10, 10, 11) sts, cont in pats to end.
Row 2 Work even in pats.

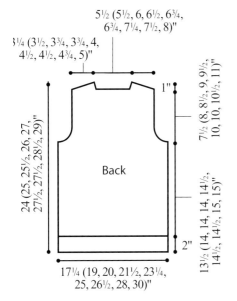

5½ (5½, 6, 6½, 6¾, 6¾, 7¼, 7½, 8)"

3¼ (3½, 3¾, 3¾, 4, 4½, 4½, 4¾, 5)"

1"

7½ (8, 8½, 9, 9½, 10, 10, 10½, 11)"

24 (25, 25½, 26, 27, 27½, 27½, 28½, 29)"

Back

13½ (14, 14, 14½, 14½, 14½, 15, 15)"

2"

17¼ (19, 20, 21½, 23¼, 25, 26½, 28, 30)"

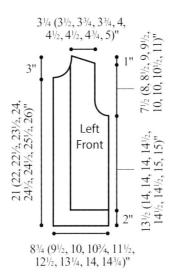

3¼ (3½, 3¾, 3¾, 4, 4½, 4½, 4¾, 5)"

3"

1"

7½ (8, 8½, 9, 9½, 10, 10, 10½, 11)"

21 (22, 22½, 23½, 24, 24½, 24½, 25½, 26)"

Left Front

13½ (14, 14, 14½, 14½, 15, 15)"

2"

8¾ (9½, 10, 10¾, 11½, 12½, 13¼, 14, 14¾)"

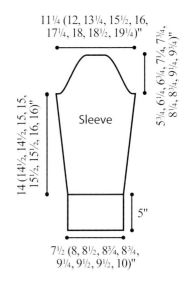

11¼ (12, 13¼, 15½, 16, 17¼, 18, 18½, 19¼)"

5¾ (6¼, 6¾, 7¼, 7¾, 8¼, 8¾, 9¼, 9¾)"

Sleeve

14 (14½, 14½, 15, 15, 15½, 15½, 16, 16)"

5"

7½ (8, 8½, 8¾, 8¾, 9¼, 9½, 9½, 10)"

Dec row 3 Bind off 2 (3, 3, 4, 4, 5, 5, 6, 6) sts, cont in pats to end.
Row 4 Work even in pats.
Dec row 5 P2, p2tog, cont in pats to end—1 st dec'd.
Row 6 Work even in pats.
Rep last 2 rows 5 (5, 5, 6, 7, 7, 10, 11, 13) times more—34 (35, 36, 38, 40, 42, 43, 45, 46) sts.
Work even in pats until armhole measures 5½ (6, 6½, 7, 7½, 8, 8, 8½, 9)"/14 (15.5, 16.5, 18, 19, 20.5, 20.5, 21.5, 23)cm, end with a WS row.

Neck and shoulder shaping

Note Neck and shoulder shaping are worked at the same time. Neck shaping is written out first, then shoulder shaping begins when same length as Back to shoulder. Keep careful track of decreases.
Next row (RS) Bind off 8 (8, 8, 9, 10, 10, 11, 12, 12) sts (neck edge), cont in pats to end.
Next row Work even in pats.
Dec row 1 (RS) K1, ssk, work to end—1 st dec'd.
Next row Work even in pats.
Rep last 2 rows 4 times more.
Next row Rep dec row 1.
Dec row 2 (WS) P to last 3 sts, p2tog tbl, p1—1 st dec'd.
Rep last 2 rows once more, then rep dec row 1 once more, AT THE SAME TIME, when same length as Back to shoulder, bind off sts from shoulder edge (beg of WS rows) as foll: bind off 4 (4, 4, 4, 5, 5, 5, 5, 6) sts at beg of next 4 (3, 2, 1, 4, 2, 2, 1, 4) WS rows, then 0 (5, 5, 5, 0, 6, 6, 6, 0) sts at beg of next 0 (1, 2, 3, 0, 2, 2, 3, 0) WS rows.

SLEEVES

Cast on 39 (41, 43, 45, 45, 47, 49, 49, 51) sts.
Row 1 (RS) *K1, p1; rep from * to last st, k1.
Row 2 P1, *k1, p1; rep from * to end.
Rep rows 1 and 2 for rib until piece measures 5"/12.5cm, and inc 1 st on last WS row—40 (42, 44, 46, 46, 48, 50, 50, 52) sts.

Begin patterns

Row 1 (RS) K15 (16, 17, 18, 18, 19, 20, 20, 21) sts, pm, work row 1 of cable panel over 10 sts, pm, k15 (16, 17, 18, 18, 19, 20, 20, 21) sts.
Row 2 P to marker, sm, work next row of cable panel over 10 sts, sm, p to end.
Row 3 K to marker, sm, work next row of cable panel over 10

sts, sm, k to end.
Cont in pats as established, and inc 1 st each side (working inc sts into St st) every 10th (8th, 8th, 4th, 4th, 4th, 4th, 4th) row 9 (3, 12, 3, 6, 10, 13, 14, 17)times, then every 0 (10th, 0, 6th, 6th, 6th, 6th, 6th) row 0 (7, 0, 14, 12, 10, 8, 8, 6)—58 (62, 68, 80, 82, 88, 92, 94, 98) sts.
Work even in pats until piece measures 14 (14½, 14½, 15, 15, 15½, 15½, 16, 16)"/36 (37, 37, 38.5, 38.5, 39.5, 39.5, 41, 41)cm above rib, end with a WS row.

Cap shaping

Cont in pats, bind off 5 (7, 8, 8, 9, 10, 10, 10, 11) sts at beg of next 2 rows, then 3 (3, 3, 4, 4, 5, 5, 6, 6) sts at beg of next 2 rows.
Cont in pats, work dec row as on Back armhole every 4th row 5 (3, 7, 7, 9, 10, 8, 10, 10) times, every 6th (6th, 6th, 2nd, 2nd, 2nd, 2nd, 2nd, 2nd) row 2 (4, 2, 7, 5, 5, 9, 7, 8) times.
Cont in pats, bind off 3 sts at beg of next 4 rows.
Bind off rem 16 sts.

FINISHING

Weave in ends. Block pieces to measurements.
Sew shoulder seams. Set in sleeves. Sew side and sleeve seams. Fold up sleeve ribbing.

Collar

Cast on 61 (61, 65, 69, 73, 73, 77, 81, 85) sts. Work in k1, p1 rib for 1 row.
Cast on 2 sts at beg of next 14 rows, working inc sts into rib—89 (89, 93, 97, 101, 101, 105, 109, 113) sts.
Work 2 rows even in rib.
Cont in rib, bind off 2 sts at beg of next 14 rows—61 (61, 65, 69, 73, 73, 77, 81, 85) sts.
Work 1 row even, then bind off in rib.
Fold collar in half with WS held tog. Sew in place around neck edge, sewing through both thicknesses.

Sew in zipper. ■

"To me, what makes someone successful is managing a healthy combination of wishing and doing."

Beautiful Day Cardigan

DESIGNED BY Carla Patrick

A cheery yellow makes the many cables on this cardigan look like rays of sunshine. An open gauge and yarn held double throughout best utilize a luxurious mohair for the perfect combination of warmth and lightness.

FINISHED MEASUREMENTS

Chest 34 (40, 45, 51, 56, 62)"/86 (104, 114, 129.5, 142, 157.5)cm
Length 24 (25, 26½, 27½, 28½, 29)"/61 (64.5, 67.5, 70, 72, 73.5)cm
Upper arm 11½ (12½, 15, 17, 18½, 19¼)"/29 (32, 38, 43, 47, 49)cm

Shown in size with 40"/104cm chest.

MATERIALS

- 8 (9, 11, 13, 15, 17) .88oz/25g balls (each approx 284yd/260m) of Berroco *Aerial* (superkid mohair/silk) in 3435 Goldenrod (4)
- One pair size 6 (4mm) needles, *or size to obtain gauges*
- Stitch markers
- Cable needle (cn)
- One separating zipper 20 (21, 22, 23, 24, 25)"/51 (54, 56, 58, 61, 64)cm long in matching color
- Sewing needle and thread in matching color

GAUGES

- 18 sts and 25 rows to 4"/10cm over St st with 2 strands of yarn held tog and using size 6 (4mm) needles.
- 28 sts and 29 rows to 4"/10cm over cable pat with 2 strands of yarn held tog and using size 6 (4mm) needles.
Take time to check gauges.

NOTE

Hold 2 strands of yarn together throughout.

CABLE PATTERN

(multiple of 10 sts plus 2)
Rows 1 and 3 (RS) *P2, k8; rep from * to last 2 sts, p2.
Row 2 and all WS rows K2, *p8, k2; rep from * to end.
Row 5 *P2, 8-st LC; rep from * to last 2 sts, p2.
Rows 7 and 9 Rep row 1.
Row 10 K2, *p8, k2; rep from * to end.
Rep rows 1–10 for cable pat.

STITCH GLOSSARY

8-st LC Sl 4 sts to cn and hold to front, k4, k4 from cn.

CARDIGAN
BACK

With 2 strands of yarn held tog, cast on 77 (91, 101, 115, 127, 141) sts.
Row 1 (RS) *K1, p1; rep from * to last st, k1.
Row 2 P1, *k1, p1; rep from * to end.
Rep last 2 rows for k1, p1 rib until piece measures 2"/5cm from beg, and dec 0 (1, 0, 0, 1, 1) st at end of last WS row—77 (90, 101, 115, 126, 140) sts.
Work even in St st (k on RS, p on WS) until piece measures 15½ (16, 16½, 16½, 17, 17)"/39.5 (40.5, 42, 42, 43, 43)cm from beg, end with a WS row.

Armhole shaping

Cont in St st, bind off 5 (7, 8, 10, 11, 12) sts at beg of next 2 rows, then 2 (3, 4, 4, 4, 5) sts at beg of next 2 (2, 2, 4, 4, 4) rows.
Dec row (RS) K2, k2tog, k to last 4 sts, ssk, k2—2 sts dec'd.
Next row Purl.
Rep last 2 rows 2 (4, 5, 4, 5, 6) times more—57 (60, 65, 69, 76, 82) sts.
Work even in St st until armhole measures 7½ (8, 9, 10, 10½, 11)"/19 (20.5, 23, 25.5, 26.5, 28)cm.

Shoulder and neck shaping

Note Shoulder and neck shaping are worked at the same time. Shoulder shaping is written out first, then neck shaping. Keep careful track of decreases.
Mark center 21 (22, 25, 25, 28, 30) sts.
Bind off 5 (5, 6, 6, 7, 8) sts at beg of next 4 (2, 6, 2, 4, 6) rows, then 6 (6, 0, 7, 8, 0) sts at beg of next 2 (4, 0, 4, 2, 0) rows, AT THE SAME TIME, on the first row of shoulder shaping, bind off center 21 (22, 25, 25, 28, 30) sts and working both sides at once with separate balls of yarn held double on both sides, bind off 2 sts from each neck edge once.

LEFT FRONT

With 2 strands of yarn held tog, cast on 58 (68, 78, 88, 98, 108) sts.

Mister Rogers loved having guests on his show to help teach children about all sorts of things. Throughout the years, he welcomed entertainers, scientists, artists, musicians, and many others. Some memorable visits included Tony Bennett, Eric Carle, Julia Child, David Copperfield, Yo-Yo Ma, and Bill Nye.

Beautiful Day Cardigan

Row 1 (RS) *K1, p1; rep from * to last 2 sts, k2.
Row 2 Sl 1, p1, *k1, p1; rep from * to end.
Rep last 2 rows for k1, p1 rib until piece measures 2"/5cm from beg, end with a WS row.

Begin cable pattern
Row 1 (RS) Work cable pat to last 6 sts, pm, [k1, p1] twice, k2 for rib.
Row 2 Sl 1, p1, [k1, p1] twice for rib, sm, work cable pat to end.
Work even in pats as established until same length as Back to armhole shaping, end with a WS row.

Armhole shaping
Dec row 1 (RS) Bind off 5 (7, 8, 10, 11, 12) sts, work pats to end.
Row 2 Work even in pats.
Cont in pats, bind off 2 (3, 4, 4, 4, 5) sts from armhole edge 2 (2, 2, 3, 4, 4) times—49 (55, 62, 66, 71, 76) sts, end with a WS row.
Dec row 2 (RS) K2, k2tog, work in pats to end—1 st dec'd.
Next row Work even in pats.
Rep last 2 rows 6 (6, 9, 7, 8, 7) times more—42 (48, 52, 58, 62, 68) sts.
Work even in pats until armhole measures 4½ (5, 6, 7, 7½, 8)"/11.5 (13, 15.5, 18, 19, 20.5)cm, end with a RS row.

Neck and shoulder shaping
Note Neck and shoulder shaping are worked at the same time. Neck shaping is written out first, then shoulder shaping begins when same length as Back to shoulder. Keep careful track of decreases.
Next row (WS) Bind off 6 (8, 9, 12, 14, 14) sts (neck edge), work cable pat to end.
Cont in cable pat, bind off 3 (3, 3, 4, 4, 4) sts from neck edge

1 (2, 3, 2, 2, 3) times, then 2 (2, 2, 2, 2, 3) sts 3 (3, 3, 3, 3, 2) times, then dec 1 st at neck edge every other row 6 (6, 5, 6, 6, 6) times, AT THE SAME TIME, when same length as Back to shoulder, bind off sts from shoulder edge (beg of RS rows), as foll: bind off 5 (6, 7, 9, 9, 10) sts once (and dec 1 (1, 1, 2, 2, 2) st in center while binding off), 8 (8, 8, 9, 9, 10) sts once (dec 2 sts evenly while binding off), and 8 (8, 8, 8, 10, 10) sts once (dec 2 sts evenly while binding off).

RIGHT FRONT
With 2 strands of yarn held tog, cast on 58 (68, 78, 88, 98, 108) sts.
Row 1 (RS) K2, *p1, k1; rep from * to end.
Row 2 *P1, k1; rep from * to last 2 sts, p1, sl 1.
Rep last 2 rows for k1, p1 rib until piece measures 2"/5cm from beg, end with a WS row.

Begin cable pattern
Row 1 (RS) K2, [p1, k1] twice for rib, work cable pat to end.
Row 2 Work in cable pat to last 6 sts, [p1, k1] twice, p1, sl 1.
Cont in pats as established until same length as Back to armhole shaping, end with a RS row.

Armhole shaping
Dec row 1 (WS) Bind off 5 (7, 8, 10, 11, 12) sts, work pats to end.
Cont in pats, bind off 2 (3, 4, 4, 4, 5) sts from armhole edge 2 (2, 2, 3, 4, 4) times—49 (55, 62, 66, 71, 76) sts, end with a WS row.
Dec row 2 (RS) Work pats to last 4 sts, ssk, k2—1 st dec'd.
Next row Work even in pats.
Rep last 2 rows 6 (6, 9, 7, 8, 7) times more—42 (48, 52, 58, 62, 68) sts.

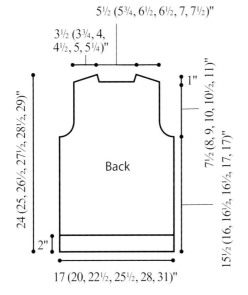

5½ (5¾, 6½, 6½, 7, 7½)"

3½ (3¾, 4, 4½, 5, 5¼)"

1"

24 (25, 26½, 27½, 28½, 29)"

7½ (8, 9, 10, 10½, 11)"

Back

15½ (16, 16½, 16½, 17, 17)"

2"

17 (20, 22½, 25½, 28, 31)"

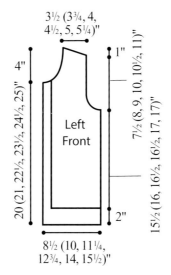

3½ (3¾, 4, 4½, 5, 5¼)"

1"

4"

20 (21, 22½, 23½, 24½, 25)"

Left Front

7½ (8, 9, 10, 10½, 11)"

15½ (16, 16½, 16½, 17, 17)"

2"

8½ (10, 11¼, 12¾, 14, 15½)"

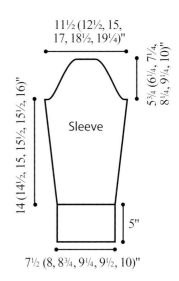

11½ (12½, 15, 17, 18½, 19¼)"

5¾ (6¼, 7¼, 8¼, 9¼, 10)"

Sleeve

14 (14½, 15, 15½, 15½, 16)"

5"

7½ (8, 8¾, 9¼, 9½, 10)"

> **"'Fame' is a four-letter word; and like 'tape' or 'zoom' or 'face' or 'pain' or 'life' or 'love,' what ultimately matters is what we do with it. I feel that those of us in television are chosen to be servants."**

Work even in pats until armhole measures 4½ (5, 6, 7, 7½, 8)"/ 11.5 (13, 15.5, 18, 19, 20.5)cm, end with a WS row.

Neck and shoulder shaping

Note Neck and shoulder shaping are worked at the same time. Neck shaping is written out first, then shoulder shaping begins when same length as Back to shoulder. Keep careful track of decreases.

Next row (RS) Bind off 6 (8, 9, 12, 14, 14) sts (neck edge), work cable pat to end.

Cont in cable pat, bind off 3 (3, 3, 4, 4, 4) sts from neck edge 1 (2, 3, 2, 2, 3) times, 2 (2, 2, 2, 2, 3) sts 3 (3, 3, 3, 3, 2) times, dec 1 st at neck edge every other row 6 (6, 5, 6, 6, 6) times, AT THE SAME TIME, when same length as Back to shoulder, work shoulder shaping at shoulder edge (beg of WS rows) as foll: bind off 5 (6, 7, 9, 9, 10) sts once (and dec 1 (1, 1, 2, 2, 2) st in center while binding off), 8 (8, 8, 9, 9, 10) sts once (dec 2 sts evenly while binding off), and 8 (8, 8, 8, 10, 10) sts once (dec 2 sts evenly while binding off).

SLEEVES

With 2 strands of yarn held tog, cast on 39 (41, 43, 45, 47, 49) sts.

Row 1 (RS) *K1, p1; rep from * to last st, k1.

Row 2 P1, *k1, p1; rep from * to end.

Rep last 2 rows for k1, p1 rib until piece measures 5"/7.5cm from beg, and inc 1 st on last WS row—40 (42, 44, 46, 48, 50) sts.

Begin cable pattern

Row 1 (RS) K14 (15, 16, 17, 18, 19) sts, pm, work row 1 of cable pat over 12 sts, pm, k14 (15, 16, 17, 18, 19) sts.

Row 2 P to marker, sm, work next row of cable pat over 12 sts, sm, p to end.

Row 3 K to marker, sm, work next row of cable pat over 12 sts, sm, k to end.

Cont in St st and cable pat as established and inc 1 st each side (working inc sts into St st) every 8th (8th, 6th, 4th, 4th, 4th) row 5 (9, 13, 10, 16, 17) times, then every 10th (10th, 8th, 6th, 6th, 6th) row 4 (1, 1, 8, 4, 4) times—58 (62, 72, 82, 88, 92) sts.

Work even in pats until piece measures 14 (14½, 15, 15½, 15½, 16)"/35.5 (37, 38, 39.5, 39.5, 40.5)cm above rib, end with a WS row.

Cap shaping

Cont in pats, bind off 5 (7, 8, 10, 11, 12) sts at beg of next 2 rows, then 2 (3, 4, 4, 4, 5) sts at beg of next 2 rows.

Cont in pats, work dec row as on Back armhole every 2nd row 4 (1, 3, 6, 7, 5) times, then every 4th row 5 (7, 8, 8, 9, 11) times.

Bind off 3 sts at beg of next 4 rows.

Bind off rem 14 sts.

FINISHING

Weave in ends. Block pieces to measurements.

Sew shoulder seams. Set in sleeves. Sew side and sleeve seams.

Collar

Cast on 57 (59, 65, 65, 71, 75) sts. Work in k1, p1 rib for 1 row.

Cast on 2 sts at beg of next 18 rows, working inc sts into rib— 93 (95, 101, 101, 107, 111) sts.

Work 2 rows even in rib.

Cont in rib, bind off 2 sts at beg of next 18 rows—57 (59, 65, 65, 71, 75) sts.

Work 1 row even, then bind off in rib.

Fold collar in half with WS held tog. Sew in place around neck edge, sewing through both thicknesses.

Sew in zipper. ∎

Junior Rogers Cardigan

DESIGNED BY Sandi Prosser

The Beautiful Day Cardigan is scaled down for children from 2 to 6 years old. This version is worked in superwash merino, rather than mohair, to ensure that it is a durable garment for even the most active of kids.

SIZES
2 years (3 years, 4 years, 5 years, 6 years).
Shown in size 5 years.

KNITTED MEASUREMENTS
Chest 25½ (26½, 27½, 28½, 30)"/65 (67.5, 70, 72.5, 76)cm
Length 14½ (16, 16½, 18, 19)"/37 (41, 42, 45.5, 48.5)cm
Upper arm 9¾ (10½, 10¾, 11, 11½)"/25 (26.5, 27.5, 28, 29)cm

MATERIALS
• 6 (7, 7, 8, 8) 1¾oz/50g balls (each approx 115yd/105m) of Jody Long *Ciao* (superwash extrafine merino wool) in #027 Primrose ⬤
• One pair each sizes 5 and 6 (3.75 and 4mm) needles, *or size to obtain gauges*
• Cable needle (cn)
• One separating zipper 12 (14, 14, 16, 16)"/30 (35, 35, 40, 40)cm long in matching color
• Sewing needle and thread in matching color

GAUGES
• 22 sts and 30 rows to 4"/10cm in St st using larger needles.
• 29 sts and 30 rows and 4"/10cm in cable pat using larger needles.
Take time to check gauges.

STITCH GLOSSARY
6-st LC Sl 3 sts to cn and hold to front, k3, k3 from cn.

CABLE PANEL
(over 6 sts)
Rows 1 and 3 (RS) Knit.
Row 2 and all WS rows Purl.
Row 5 6-st LC.
Row 7 Knit.
Row 8 Purl
Rep rows 1–8 for cable panel.

CARDIGAN
BACK
With larger needles, cast on 75 (77, 81, 83, 89) sts.
Row 1 (RS) K1, *k1, p1; rep from * to last 2 sts, k2.
Row 2 *K1, p1; rep from * to last st, k1.
Rep last 2 rows for k1, p1 rib until piece measures 1½"/4cm, end with a RS row.
Dec row (WS) Work in rib and dec 5 (4, 5, 5, 6) sts evenly across—70 (73, 76, 78, 83) sts.
Work even in St st (k on RS, p on WS) until piece measures 9 (10, 10½, 11½, 12)"/23 (25.5, 26.5, 29, 30.5)cm from beg, end with a WS row.

Armhole shaping
Cont in St st, bind off 4 sts at beg of next 2 rows—62 (65, 68, 70, 75) sts.
Dec 1 st each end of next 3 rows, then every RS row twice—52 (55, 58, 60, 65) sts.
Work even in St st until armhole measures 5 (5½, 5½, 6, 6½)"/12.5 (14, 14, 15, 16.5)cm, end with a WS row.

Shoulder shaping
Cont in St st, bind off 6 (6, 7, 7, 8) sts at beg of next 2 rows, then 6 (7, 7, 8, 9) sts at beg of next 2 rows.
Bind off rem 28 (29, 30, 30, 31) sts for back neck.

LEFT FRONT
With larger needles, cast on 41 (43, 43, 45, 47) sts.
Row 1 (RS) K1, *p1, k1; rep from * to end.
Row 2 K1, *k1, p1; rep from * to last 2 sts, k2.
Rep last 2 rows for k1, p1 rib until piece measures 1½"/4cm, end with a RS row.
Inc row (WS) Work in rib and inc 3 (3, 5, 5, 5) sts evenly across—44 (46, 48, 50, 52) sts.

Cable pattern
Row 1 (RS) K5 (7, 1, 3, 5), *p2, work row 1 of cable panel over next 6 sts; rep from * to last 7 sts, p2, k3, p1, k1.

Mister Rogers kept every drawing and letter he received, and he made it a part of his daily routine to respond to every piece of fan mail from his young viewers. Each response was personalized and never a form letter.

Junior Rogers Cardigan

Row 2 K2, p3, *k2, work next row of cable panel over next 6 sts; rep from * to last 7 (9, 3, 5, 7) sts, k2, p5 (7, 1, 3, 5). Rep last 2 rows for cable pat until piece measures 9 (10, 10½, 11½, 12)"/23 (25.5, 26.5, 29, 30.5)cm from beg, end with a WS row.

Armhole shaping

Cont in pat as foll:
Bind off 4 sts at beg of next RS row—40 (42, 44, 46, 48) sts.
Dec 1 st at armhole edge on next 5 rows, then every RS row 3 times—32 (34, 36, 38, 40) sts.
Work even until armhole measures 2½ (3, 3, 3½, 4)"/6.5 (7.5, 7.5, 9, 10)cm, end with a RS row.

Neck and shoulder shaping

Note Neck and shoulder shaping are worked at the same time. Neck shaping is written out first, then shoulder shaping begins when same length as Back to shoulder. Keep careful track of decreases.
Dec row 1 (WS) Bind off 4 sts, work in pat to end—28 (30, 32, 34, 36) sts.
Row 2 Work even in pat.
Dec row 3 Bind off 3 sts, work in pat to end—25 (27, 29, 31, 33) sts.
Cont in pat, dec 1 st at neck edge on next 7 rows, then at neck edge every RS row 2 (3, 3, 4, 4) times, AT THE SAME TIME, when armhole measures same as Back to shoulder, bind off from shoulder edge 8 (8, 9, 10, 11) sts once, then bind off rem 8 (9, 10, 10, 11) sts.

RIGHT FRONT

Work as for Left Front until cable pat.

Cable pattern

Row 1 (RS) K1, p1, k3, *p2, work row 1 of cable panel over next 6 sts; rep from * to last 7 (9, 3, 5, 7) sts, p2, k5 (7, 1, 3, 5).
Row 2 P5 (7, 1, 3, 5), *k2, work next row of cable panel over next 6 sts; rep from * to last 7 sts, k2, p3, k2.
Rep last 2 rows for cable pat until piece measures 9 (10, 10½, 11½, 12)"/23 (25.5, 26.5, 29, 30.5)cm from beg, end with a RS row.

Armhole shaping

Cont in pat, as foll:
Bind off 4 sts at beg of next WS row—40 (42, 44, 46, 48) sts.
Dec 1 st at armhole edge on next 5 rows, then every RS row 3 times—32 (34, 36, 38, 40) sts.
Work even until armhole measures 2½ (3, 3, 3½, 4)"/6.5 (7.5, 7.5, 9, 10)cm, end with a WS row.

Neck and shoulder shaping

Note Neck and shoulder shaping are worked at the same time. Neck shaping is written out first, then shoulder shaping begins when same length as Back to shoulder. Keep careful track of decreases.
Dec row 1 (RS) Bind off 4 sts, work in pat to end—28 (30, 32, 34, 36) sts.
Row 2 Work even in pat.
Dec row 3 Bind off 3 sts, work in pat to end—25 (27, 29, 31, 33) sts.
Cont in pat, dec 1 st at neck edge on next 7 rows, then at neck edge every RS row 2 (3, 3, 4, 4) times, AT THE SAME TIME, when armhole measures same as Back to shoulder, bind off from shoulder edge 8 (8, 9, 10, 11) sts once, then bind off rem 8 (9, 10, 10, 11) sts.

SLEEVES

With smaller needles, cast on 37 (37, 39, 39, 41) sts.
Row 1 (RS) K1, *k1, p1; rep from * to last 2 sts, k2.
Row 2 *K1, p1; rep from * to last st, k1.

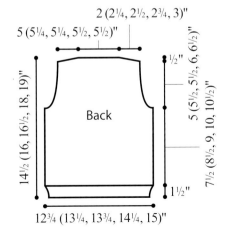

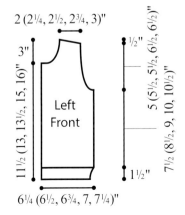

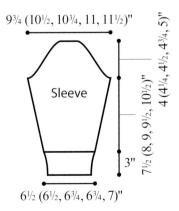

Rep rows 1 and 2 for k1, p1 rib until piece measures 3"/7.5cm, end with a RS row.
Inc row (WS) Work in rib and inc 3 sts evenly across—40 (40, 42, 42, 44) sts.

Cable panel
Change to larger needles.
Row 1 (RS) K15 (15, 16, 16, 17), p2, work row 1 of cable panel over next 6 sts, p2, k15 (15, 16, 16, 17).
Row 2 P15 (15, 16, 16, 17), k2, work next row of cable panel over next 6 sts, k2, p15 (15, 16, 16, 17).
Cont in St st and cable panel as established for 2 rows more, then inc 1 st each side on next row and every 6th row 4 (4, 7, 8, 10) times more, then every 4th row 4 (6, 3, 2, 1) times, working inc sts into St st—58 (62, 64, 66, 68) sts.
Work even in pats until piece measures 10½ (11, 12, 12½, 13½)"/26.5 (28, 30.5, 32, 34.5)cm from beg, end with a WS row.

Cap shaping
Cont in pats as foll:
Bind off 4 sts at beg of next 2 rows—50 (54, 56, 58, 60) sts.
Dec 1 st at each side on next 5 rows, then every RS row 9 (9, 10, 11, 12) times, end with a WS row—22 (26, 26, 26, 26) sts.
Dec 1 st at each side on next 3 (5, 5, 5, 5) rows—16 sts.
Work 1 row even.
Bind off rem sts.

FINISHING
Weave in ends. Lightly block to measurements.
Sew shoulder seams. Set in sleeves. Sew side and sleeve seams, reversing seaming 2"/5cm from sleeve cast-on edge to allow for turnback.

Collar
With smaller needles, cast on 41 (41, 43, 43, 45) sts.
Set-up row (WS) K1, *p1, k1; rep from * to end.
Cast on 4 sts at beg of next 10 rows, working inc sts into rib—81 (81, 83, 83, 85) sts.

Work 2 rows even in rib.
Cont in rib, bind off 4 sts at beg of next 10 rows—41 (41, 43, 43, 45) sts.
Bind off rem sts.

With RS facing, sew one long edge of Collar to neck edge, easing collar to fit.
Sew zipper in place along front edges, having top of zipper meet start of neck shaping and adjusting zipper length as required.
Fold collar in half to WS and sew rem long edge in place (hiding zipper tape). ■

"Anyone who does anything to help a child in his life is a hero."

Baby Rogers Cardigan

DESIGNED BY Sandi Prosser

Baby showers and first and second birthdays will be extra special when the little one receives his or her very own mini-version of Mister Rogers' Beginnings Cardigan. The raglan shaping and ribbed sleeves make for an extra snuggly fit.

SIZES
6 months (12 months, 18 months, 24 months).
Shown in size 12 months.

KNITTED MEASUREMENTS
Chest 20 (22½, 23½, 24½)"/51 (57, 60, 62)cm
Length 10 (11½, 12½, 13½)"/25.5 (29, 32, 34.5)cm
Upper arm 9 (9½, 9¾, 10¼)"/23 (24, 25, 26)cm

MATERIALS
• 1 (2, 2, 2) 3½oz/100g balls (each approx 400yd/366m) of Berroco *Ultra Wool Fine* (superwash wool) in 53122 Sunflower (1)
• One pair each size 3 and 4 (3.25 and 3.5mm) needles, *or size to obtain gauge*
• One separating zipper 10 (10, 12, 12)"/25 (25, 30, 30)cm long in matching color
• Sewing needle and thread in matching color

GAUGE
26 sts and 34 rows to 4"/10cm in St st using larger needles.
Take time to check gauge.

CARDIGAN
BACK
With smaller needles, cast on 70 (78, 82, 86) sts.
Row 1 (RS) K2, *p2, k2; rep from * to end.
Row 2 P2, *k2, p2; rep from * to end.
Rep last 2 rows until piece measures 1"/2.5cm, end with a WS row and dec 4 (5, 4, 6) sts evenly across last row—66 (73, 76, 80) sts.
Change to larger needles and work even in St st (k on RS, p on WS) until piece measures 6 (6¾, 7½, 8)"/15 (17, 19, 20)cm from beg, end with a WS row.

Raglan shaping
Cont in St st, bind off 4 sts at beg of next 2 rows—58 (65, 68, 72) sts.
Work even for 0 (0, 2, 2) rows more.
Dec row 1 (RS) K1, k2tog, k to last 3 sts, SKP, k1—2 sts dec'd.

Row 2 K1, p to last st, k1.
Rep last 2 rows 16 (19, 19, 21) times more—24 (25, 28, 28) sts.
Bind off rem sts for back neck.

LEFT FRONT
With smaller needles, cast on 34 (38, 38, 42) sts.
Row 1 (RS) K2, *p2, k2; rep from * to end.
Row 2 P2, *k2, p2; rep from * to end.
Rep last 2 rows until piece measures 1"/2.5cm, end with a WS row and dec 2 (2, 1, 3) sts evenly across—32 (36, 37, 39) sts.
Change to larger needles and work even in St st until piece measures 6 (6¾, 7½, 8)"/15 (17, 19, 20)cm from beg, end with a WS row.

Raglan shaping
Cont in St st, bind off 4 sts at beg of next row—28 (32, 33, 35) sts.
Work even for 1 (1, 3, 3) row(s) more.
Dec row 1 (RS) K1, k2tog, k to end—1 st dec'd.
Row 2 K1, p to last st, k1.
Rep last 2 rows 10 (13, 13, 15) times more, then rep dec row 1 once more—16 (17, 18, 18) sts.
Cont raglan shaping and beg neck shaping as foll:
Dec row 1 (WS) Bind off 3 (4, 5, 5) sts, p to last st, k1—13 sts.
Dec row 2 K1, k2tog, k to end—12 sts.
Dec row 3 Bind off 3 sts, p to last st, k1—9 sts.
Dec row 4 K1, k2tog, k to last 3 sts, SKP, k1—7 sts.
Rows 5 and 7 K1, p to last st, k1.
Dec row 6 K1, k2tog, k to last 3 sts, SKP, k1—5 sts.
Dec row 8 K1, k3tog, k1—3 sts.
Row 9 K1, p1, k1.
Dec row 10 K1, k2tog—2 sts.
Row 11 Purl.
Dec row 12 K2tog and fasten off rem st.

RIGHT FRONT
Work as for Left Front to raglan shaping but end with a RS row.

Raglan shaping
Cont in St st, bind off 4 sts at beg of next row—28 (32, 33, 35) sts.
Work even for 1 (1, 3, 3) row(s) more.

Mister Rogers influenced his viewers and also other television shows. Marc Brown, creator of Arthur, considered Mister Rogers a good friend and role model. Similarly, Josh Selig, creator of Wonder Pets, and Angela Santomero, co-creator of Blue's Clues, both credit Mister Rogers as an inspiration and influence.

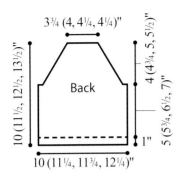

Back

3¾ (4, 4¼, 4¼)"

10 (11½, 12½, 13½)"

4 (4¾, 5, 5½)"

5 (5¾, 6½, 7)"

1"

10 (11¼, 11¾, 12¼)"

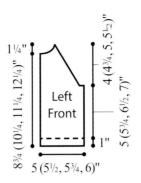

Left Front

1¼"

8¾ (10¼, 11¼, 12¼)"

4 (4¾, 5, 5½)"

5 (5¾, 6½, 7)"

1"

5 (5½, 5¾, 6)"

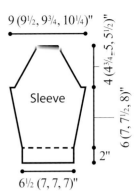

Sleeve

9 (9½, 9¾, 10¼)"

4 (4¾, 5, 5½)"

6 (7, 7½, 8)"

2"

6½ (7, 7, 7)"

Dec row 1 (RS) K to last 3 sts, SKP, k1.

Row 2 K1, p to last st, k1.

Rep last 2 rows 10 (13, 13, 15) times more—17 (18, 19, 19) sts.

Cont raglan shaping and beg neck shaping as foll:

Dec row 1 (RS) Bind off 3 (4, 5, 5) sts, k to last 3 sts, SKP, k1—13 sts.

Row 2 K1, p to last st, k1.

Dec row 3 Bind off 3 sts, k to last 3 sts, SKP, k1—9 sts.

Rows 4, 6, and 8 K1, p to last st, k1.

Dec row 5 K1, k2tog, k to last 3 sts, SKP, k1—7 sts.

Dec row 7 K1, k2tog, k1, SKP, k1—5 sts.

Dec row 9 K1, k3tog tbl, k1—3 sts.

Row 10 K1, p1, k1.

Dec row 11 SKP, k1—2 sts.

Row 12 Purl.

Dec row 13 K2tog and fasten off rem st.

SLEEVES

With smaller needles, cast on 42 (46, 46, 46) sts.

Row 1 (RS) K2, *p2, k2; rep from * to end.

Row 2 P2, *k2, p2; rep from * to end.

Rep last 2 rows until piece measures 2"/5cm, end with a RS row.

Inc row (WS) Rib 9 (11, 11, 11), [M1, rib 8] 3 times, M1, rib to end—46 (50, 50, 50) sts.

Change to larger needles.

Row 1 (RS) K8 (10, 10, 10), [p3, k6] 3 times, p3, k8 (10, 10, 10).

Row 2 P8 (10, 10, 10), [k3, p6] 3 times, k3, p8 (10, 10, 10).

Rep last 2 rows once more.

Cont in pat as established and inc 1 st at each side of next and every foll 4th row 3 (0, 0, 0) times, then every 6th row 5 (8, 9, 10) times, working inc sts into St st—64 (68, 70, 72) sts.

Work even in pats until piece measures 8 (9, 9½, 10)"/20 (23, 24, 25.5)cm from beg, end with a WS row.

Raglan shaping

Cont in pat, bind off 4 sts at beg of next 2 rows—56 (60, 62, 64) sts.

Work even for 0 (0, 0, 2) rows more.

Size 6 months only

Dec row 1 (RS) K1, k2tog, work to last 3 sts, SKP, k1.

Dec row 2 K1, p2tog tbl, work to last 3 sts, p2tog, k1—52 sts.

All sizes

Dec row 1 (RS) K1, k2tog, work to last 3 sts, SKP, k1.

Row 2 K1, work to last st, k1.

Rep last 2 rows 16 (19, 20, 21) times more—18 (20, 20, 20) sts.

Bind off rem sts.

FINISHING

Weave in ends. Lightly block pieces to measurements.

Sew raglan sleeve caps into raglan armholes. Sew side and sleeve seams, reversing seaming 1¼"/3cm from sleeve cast-on edge to allow for rib turnback.

Front edgings

With RS facing and larger needles, pick up and k 65 (75, 82, 89) sts evenly along Left Front edge. Bind off all sts knitwise.

With RS facing and larger needles, pick up and k 65 (75, 82, 89) sts evenly along Right Front edge. Bind off all sts knitwise.

Collar

With smaller needles, cast on 50 (54, 58, 58) sts.

Set-up row (WS) P2, *k2, p2; rep from * to end.

Cast on 4 sts at beg of next 10 rows, working inc sts into rib—90 (94, 98, 98) sts.

Work 2 rows even in rib.

Cont in rib, bind off 4 sts at beg of next 10 rows—50 (54, 58, 58) sts.

Bind off rem sts.

With RS facing, sew one long edge of Collar to neck edge, easing collar to fit.

Sew zipper in place along front edges, having top of zipper meet start of neck shaping and adjusting zipper length as required. Fold collar in half to WS and sew rem long edge in place (hiding zipper tape). ■

Baby Rogers Onesie

DESIGNED BY Sandi Prosser

There aren't many things cuter than this faux-cardigan onesie. Baby will be free to crawl, walk, and run with minimal fuss. Buttons along the inseam help with easy changes, and a wool/nylon blend make this adorable outfit incredibly durable.

■■■▶

SIZES
6 months (12 months, 18 months, 24 months).
Shown in size 12 months.

KNITTED MEASUREMENTS
Chest 20 (22½, 24, 25½)"/51 (57, 61, 65)cm
Length 17¼ (18¾, 20½, 21¾)"/44 (47.5, 52, 55)cm
Upper arm 8 (8¾, 9½, 10)"/20 (22, 24, 25.5)cm
Inseam 2¾ (3¼, 3¾, 4)"/7 (8, 9.5, 10)cm

MATERIALS
• 2 (2, 3, 3) 1¾oz/50g balls (each approx 191yd/175m) of Sandnes Garn *Sisu* (wool/nylon) in 8031 Chinos Green (A) ❶
• 2 (2, 3, 3) balls 7562 Green (B)
• One pair each sizes 2 and 3 (2.75 and 3.25mm) needles, *or size to obtain gauge*
• Stitch holders
• Removable stitch markers
• Cable needle (cn)
• Ten ½"/13mm buttons

GAUGE
28 sts and 36 rows to 4"/10cm over St st using larger needles.
Take time to check gauge.

STITCH GLOSSARY
6-st LC Sl next 3 sts to cn and hold to front, k3, k3 from cn.

CABLE PANEL
(over 10 sts)
Rows 1 and 3 (RS) P2, k6, p2.
Row 2 and all WS rows K2, p6, k2.

Row 5 P2, 6-st LC, p2.
Row 7 P2, k6, p2.
Row 8 K2, p6, k2.
Rep rows 1–8 for cable panel.

K1, P1 RIB
(over an odd number of sts)
Row 1 (RS) K1, *p1, k1; rep from * to end.
Row 2 P1, *k1, p1; rep from * to end.
Rep rows 1 and 2 for K1, P1 rib.

ONESIE
BACK
Left leg
With smaller needles and A, cast on 37 (41, 43, 45) sts.
Work 4 rows in k1, p1 rib and inc 2 sts evenly across last row—39 (43, 45, 47) sts.
Change to larger needles.
Beg with a RS row, work in St st (k on RS, p on WS) and inc 1 st at beg of 5th row and then every 4th row 4 (4, 5, 5) times—44 (48, 51, 53) sts.
Work even until piece measures 2¾ (3¼, 3¾, 4)"/7 (8, 9.5,10)cm, end with a WS row. Cut yarn and place sts on holder.

Right leg
With smaller needles and A, cast on 37 (41, 43, 45) sts.
Work 4 rows in k1, p1 rib and inc 2 sts evenly across last row—39 (43, 45, 47) sts.
Change to larger needles.
Beg with a RS row, work in St st and inc 1 st at end of 5th row and then every 4th row 4 (4, 5, 5) times—44 (48, 51, 53) sts.
Work even until piece measures 2¾ (3¼, 3¾, 4)"/7 (8, 9.5, 10)cm, end with a WS row. Do not cut yarn.
Joining row (RS) K43 (47, 50, 52) sts from right leg, pm, k last st of right leg and first st of left leg tog (this becomes center st), pm, k43 (47, 50, 52) sts from left leg—87 (95, 101, 105) sts.

Mister Rogers is best known for his television show, but he was also a published author. He wrote books for children that span a wide range of topics such as potty training, making friends, and even coping with the death of a family pet.

"*Discovering the truth about ourselves is a lifetime's work, but it's worth the effort.*"

Next row Purl.
Dec row 1 (RS) K to 2 sts before first center st marker, SKP, sm, k1, sm, k2tog, k to end—2 sts dec'd.
Row 2 Purl.
Rep last 2 rows 3 (4, 4, 4) times more—79 (85, 91, 95) sts.**
Work even in St st until piece measures 4¾ (5½, 6¼, 7)"/12 (14, 16, 18)cm from joining row, end with a WS row and pm at each end of last row.
Work even for 14 rows, end with a WS row.

Side shaping
Cont in St st, dec 1 st each side of next row and then every 12th row twice—73 (79, 85, 89) sts.
Work even in St st until piece measures 10¼ (11, 11¾, 12½)"/26 (28, 30, 32)cm from joining row, end with a WS row.

Armhole shaping
Cont in St st, bind off 4 sts at beg of next 2 rows, 1 st each side of next 3 (5, 5, 5) rows, and then 1 st each side every RS row twice—55 (57, 63, 67) sts.
Work even in St st until armhole measures 4¼ (4½, 5, 5¼)"/11 (11.5, 12.5, 13.5)cm, end with a WS row.
Bind off all sts.

FRONT
Right front rib
With larger needles and B, cast on 45 (49, 55, 57) sts.
Row 1 (RS) Sl 1 wyif, k2, *p1, k1; rep from * to end.
Row 2 P1, *k1, p1; rep from * to last 2 sts, p1, k1.
Rep last 2 rows 4 times more, end with a WS row and dec 1 st at center of last row—44 (48, 54, 56) sts.
Place sts on spare needle, ready to work a RS row. Do not cut yarn. Set aside.

Left front rib
With larger needles and B, cast on 45 (49, 55, 57) sts.
Row 1 (RS) *K1, p1; rep from * to last 3 sts, k2, p1.
Row 2 Sl 1 wyif, p2, *k1, p1; rep from * to end.
Rep last 2 rows twice more, end with a WS row.
Buttonhole row (RS) Rib to last 6 sts, p2tog, yo, p1, k3.
Work 3 rows even in rib, end with a WS row and dec 1 st at center of last row—44 (48, 54, 56) sts.
Place sts on spare needle, ready to work a RS row. Do not cut yarn. Set aside.

Legs
Work as for Back to **.
Work even in St st until piece measures 4¾ (5½, 6¼, 7)"/12 (14, 16, 18)cm from joining row, end with a RS row.

Divide for front opening
Next row (WS) P36 (40, 43, 45), turn and leave rem sts on holder. Cut yarn.

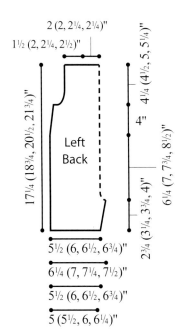

2 (2, 2¼, 2¼)"
1½ (2, 2¼, 2½)"
4¼ (4½, 5, 5¼)"
4"
6¼ (7, 7¾, 8½)"
17¼ (18¾, 20½, 21¾)"
Left Back
2¾ (3¼, 3¾, 4)"
5½ (6, 6½, 6¾)"
6¼ (7, 7¼, 7½)"
5½ (6, 6½, 6¾)"
5 (5½, 6, 6¼)"

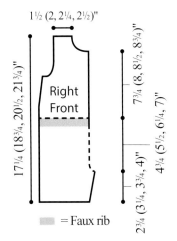

1½ (2, 2¼, 2½)"
7¾ (8, 8½, 8¾)"
17¼ (18¾, 20½, 21¾)"
Right Front
4¾ (5½, 6¼, 7)"
2¾ (3¼, 3¾, 4)"
= Faux rib

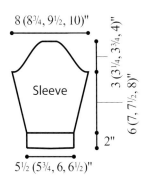

8 (8¾, 9½, 10)"
3 (3¼, 3¾, 4)"
Sleeve
6 (7, 7½, 8)"
2"
5½ (5¾, 6, 6½)"

Right front

Cont on these 36 (40, 43, 45) sts only for right front as foll:
Hold right front rib and right front tog with needles parallel and rib in front, ready to work a RS row.
With larger needles and B, work first 6 sts of rib, insert RH needle knitwise into next st of rib and first st of right front and knit them tog, *insert RH needle knitwise into next st of both rib and right front and knit them tog; rep from * 4 times more, [k1 from rib, knit 1 st tog from rib and right front] 2 (2, 5, 5) times, *knit 1 st tog from rib and right front; rep from * to end—44 (48, 54, 56) sts.

Next row (WS) P27 (31, 37, 39), work row 2 of cable panel over next 10 sts, rib to end.

Next row Rib 7, work row 3 of cable panel over next 10 sts, k to end.
Work even in pats as established for 11 rows more, working appropriate row of cable panel, and end with a WS row.

Side shaping

Cont in pats, dec 1 st at end of next RS row and then every 12th RS row twice—41 (45, 51, 53) sts.
Work even in pats until piece measures same as Back to armhole, end with a RS row.

Armhole shaping

Cont in pats, bind off 4 sts at beg of next WS row (armhole edge)—37 (41, 47, 49) sts.

Cont in pats, dec 1 st at each armhole edge of next 3 (5, 5, 5) rows, then every RS row twice—32 (34, 40, 42) sts.
Work even in pats until 18 rows less than Back have been worked, end with a WS row.

Neck shaping

Cont in pats, bind off 7 (7, 9, 9) sts at beg of next RS row (neck edge), and then bind off 3 (3, 5, 5) sts at beg of foll RS row.
Cont in pats, dec 1 st at neck edge of next 8 rows, and then every RS row twice—12 (14, 16, 18) sts.
Work 3 rows even in pat. Bind off rem sts.
Mark position for 4 further buttons (first button is 6 rows from cast-on edge of rib), having top button ½"/1cm from start of neck shaping and rem 3 spaced evenly between.

With WS facing, return to front sts on hold, rejoin yarn and bind off center 5 sts, p to end—36 (40, 43, 45) sts.

Left front

Hold left front rib and left front tog with needles parallel and rib in front, ready for a RS row.
With larger needles and B, *insert RH needle knitwise into first st of both rib and left front and knit them tog; rep from * to last 14 (14, 20, 20) sts of rib, [k1 from rib, knit 1 st tog from rib and right front] 2 (2, 5, 5) times, [knit 1 st tog from rib and right front] 3 times, rib last 7 sts of rib—44 (48, 54, 56) sts.

Next row (WS) Rib 7 sts, work row 2 of cable panel over next 10 sts, p to end.

Next row K27 (31, 37, 39), work row 3 of cable panel over next 10 sts, rib to end.

Work even as established for 11 rows, working buttonholes to correspond to markers on right front, and end with a WS row.

Side shaping

Cont in pats, dec 1 st at beg of next RS row and then every 12th RS row twice—41 (45, 51, 53) sts.

Work even in pats until piece measures same as Back to armhole, end with a WS row.

Armhole shaping

Cont in pats, bind off 4 sts at beg of next RS row (armhole edge)—37 (41, 47, 49) sts.

Work 1 row even.

Cont in pats, dec 1 st at each armhole edge on next 3 (5, 5, 5) rows, then every RS row twice—32 (34, 40, 42) sts.

Work even until 19 rows less than Back have been worked, end with a RS row.

Neck Shaping

Cont in pats, bind off 7 (7, 9, 9) sts at beg of next WS row (neck edge), and then bind off 3 (3, 5, 5) sts at beg of next WS row.

Cont in pats, dec 1 st at neck edge on next 8 rows, and then every RS row twice—12 (14, 16, 18) sts.

Work 4 rows even. Bind off rem sts.

SLEEVES

With smaller needles and B, cast on 39 (41, 43, 45) sts.

Work in k1, p1 rib for 2"/5cm, end with a WS row.

Change to larger needles.

Beg with a RS row, work in St st and inc 1 st at each end of the 5th and then every foll 6th row 7 (9, 11, 12) times—55 (61, 67, 71) sts.

Work even in St st until piece measures 8 (9, 9½, 10)"/20 (23, 24, 25.5)cm from beg, end with a WS row.

Cap shaping

Cont in St st as foll:

Bind off 4 sts at beg of next 2 rows—47 (53, 59, 63) sts.

Dec 1 st at each end of next 3 (5, 5, 7) rows, then every RS row 8 (8, 9, 9) times, end with a WS row—25 (27, 31, 31) sts.

Dec 1 st at each end of next 5 (5, 7, 7) rows—15 (17, 17, 17) sts.

Work 1 row even. Bind off rem sts.

FINISHING

Weave in ends. Block lightly to measurements.

Sew shoulder seams.

Collar

With smaller needles and B, cast on 39 (39, 43, 43) sts.

Set-up row (WS) K1, *p1, k1; rep from * to end.

Cast on 4 sts at beg of next 12 rows, working inc sts into rib—87 (87, 91, 91) sts.

Work 2 rows even in rib.

Cont in rib, bind off 4 sts at beg of next 12 rows—39 (39, 43, 43) sts.

Bind off rem sts.

Front leg band

Note In this section, "rib2tog" means to either k2tog or p2tog, however you believe will look best in the established rib.

With smaller needles, RS facing and A, pick up and k 24 (26, 28, 30) sts evenly along edge of front right leg and 24 (26, 28, 30) sts evenly along edge of front left leg—48 (52, 56, 60) sts.

Work 2 rows in k1, p1 rib.

Buttonhole row (WS) Rib 3, [yo, rib2tog, rib 8 (9, 10, 11)] 4 times, yo, rib2tog, rib 3.

Work 1 row even in rib.

Bind off in rib.

Back leg band

With smaller needles, RS facing and A, pick up and k 24 (26, 28, 30) sts evenly along edge of back left leg and 24 (26, 28, 30) sts along front edge of right leg—48 (52, 56, 60) sts.

Work 4 rows even in k1, p1 rib.

Bind off in rib.

Set in sleeves.

Sew side and sleeve seams, matching marker on back to joining row of rib on front and reversing last 1¼"/3cm of sleeve cuff for rib turnback.

With RS facing, starting and ending at middle of front button/buttonhole bands, sew one long edge of Collar to neck edge, easing collar to fit. Fold collar in half to WS and sew rem long edge in place.

Sew bound-off sts of front opening to WS of front button band.

Sew buttons to back leg band opposite buttonholes. Sew buttons to front opening button band opposite buttonholes. ∎

"I hope you're proud of yourself for the times you've said 'yes,' when all it meant was extra work for you and was seemingly helpful only to someone else."

Puppets

The Neighborhood of Make-Believe is never far when you knit up some of its most memorable characters. Each puppet is knit with a similar body construction. Watch them come to life as you add whimsical details.

Daniel Striped Tiger Puppet

DESIGNED BY Nicky Epstein

Worked mostly in the round, this puppet is whipped up quickly in a single yarn.
The stripes, whiskers, ears, face embroidery, eyes, and even a tiny watch
are added to make Daniel come alive.

FINISHED MEASUREMENTS
Height 13"/33cm

MATERIALS
- 1 6½oz/184g skein (approx 89yd/81m) of Lion Brand *Go For Fleece Sherpa* (polyester) each in #158 Honey (A) and #124 Clay (B) 🄦
- One pair size 15 (10mm) needles, *or size to obtain gauge*
- Small amount of DK- or worsted-weight yarn in brown, black, and red (for mouth, paws, and nose)
- Two plastic green cat eye buttons
- Tapestry needle
- Small amount of polyester stuffing
- Small wrist watch

GAUGE
10 sts and 13 rows to 4"/10cm over rev St st using size 15 (10mm) needles.
Take time to check gauge.

NOTE
Before you begin, cut 2 lengths of A, each approx 36"/91.5cm long, to be used when working the body in 3 sections at the same time.

PUPPET
BODY
With A, cast on 29 sts. Work rev St st (p on RS, k on WS) for 6"/15cm, end with a RS row.
Next row (WS) K6 (6 sts for half back), bind off next 3 sts, k10 (11 sts for front), bind off next 3 sts, k to end (6 sts for half back). Work each section with a separate length of yarn as foll:
Next 3 rows Purl 1 row, knit 1 row, purl 1 row.
Dec row K2, k2tog, k2 (5 sts for half back); k11 (for front); k2, k2tog, k2 (5 sts for half back).

Next row Purl across each section.
Cont with a single ball of yarn, closing gaps between sections.
Join/dec row (WS) K2, k2tog, k to last 3 sts, k2tog, k1—19 sts.
Next row Purl.
Next row K1, k2tog, k to last 3 sts, k2tog, k1—17 sts.

Shape Neck
Cont in rev St st, bind off 3 sts at beg of next 2 rows—11 sts.

HEAD
Shape Nose
Inc row 1 (RS) P2, [pfb] 7 times, p2 —18 sts.
Inc row 2 K8, [kfb] twice, k8—20 sts.
Rows 3 and 5 Purl.
Inc row 4 K9, [kfb] twice, k9—22 sts.
Dec row 6 K9, [k2tog] twice, k9—20 sts.
Rows 7–9 Cont in rev St st, work 3 rows even.
Dec row 10 K1, [k2tog] 9 times, k1—11 sts.
Row 11 Purl.
Row 12 K1, [k2tog] 5 times—6 sts. Bind off.

ARMS
With A, cast on 4 sts. Work in rev St st as foll:
Inc 1 st at beg of next 2 rows—6 sts.
Work 4 rows even.
Inc 1 st at beg of next 2 rows—8 sts.
Work even until piece measures 4"/10cm from beg.
Bind off loosely.

EARS
With A, cast on 4 sts.
Row 1 Knit
Row 2 Purl.
Dec row 3 [K2tog] twice, pass 2nd st over first st and secure rem st.

Some might be surprised to learn that Mister Rogers was a naturally shy person. When asked which puppet he most identified with, he said it was Daniel Striped Tiger, who is known for being timid.

Daniel Striped Tiger Puppet

FINISHING

Sew back seam of body.

Stripes

Cut strands of B at various lengths and sew to back, arms and face for stripes (see photos for inspiration).

Sew side seams of arms. Sew arms into openings along body. Sew back of head seam. Lightly stuff head.

Sew on ears. Attach eyes to face. Embroider mouth, nose (shape nose by squeezing), and paws (see photos). ∎

"We speak with more than our mouths.
We listen with more than our ears."

King Friday the XIII Puppet

DESIGNED by Nicky Epstein

Lavish details give this puppet the royal treatment. Begin with a seed stitch robe, then move on to a faux-fur-trimmed cape, further embellished with tassels. Buttons, jewel-like beads, and a chain are added for extra dimension.

FINISHED MEASUREMENTS
Height 12"/30.5cm

MATERIALS
- 1 5oz/142g skein (approx 251yd/230m) of Lion Brand *Heartland* (acrylic/rayon) in #105 Glacier Bay (A)
- 1 3½oz/100g skein (approx 185yd/170m) of Lion Brand *Basic Stitch Anti Pilling* (acrylic) in #409 Blush Heather (B)
- 1 3oz/85g skein (approx 197yd/180m) of Lion Brand *Wool-Ease* (acrylic/wool) each in #099 Fisherman (C) and #047 Raindrops (D)
- Approx ½yd/91.5cm of Lion Brand *Go For Faux Thick & Quick* in #098 Baked Alaska (E)
- One gold mini-skein from one package of Lion Brand *Bonbons* in #650 Party (F)
- One pair each sizes 4, 6, and 8 (3.5, 4, and 5mm) needles, *or size to obtain gauges*
- Tapestry needle
- 8 small white pearls
- 5 small blue beads
- 6 small flower-shaped buttons
- ½yd/.5m of gold metallic fringe trim
- 3"/7.5cm length of small gold chain
- Small amount of polyester stuffing
- Pink embroidery floss
- Small quantity of fine black yarn

GAUGES
- 16 sts and 18 rows to 4"/10cm over St st using D and size 8 (5mm) needles.
- 16 sts and 28 rows to 4"/10cm over seed st using A and size 8 (5mm) needles.
Take time to check gauges.

SEED STITCH
(over an odd number of sts)
Row 1 K1 *p1, k1; rep from * to end.
Rep row 1 for seed st.

NOTE
Before you begin, wind 2 small balls of A to be used when working the gown in 3 sections at the same time.

PUPPET
GOWN
With A and size 8 (5mm) needles, cast on 47 sts. Work even in seed st for 6½"/16.5cm, end with a WS row.
Next row (RS) Work 14 sts (14 sts for half back), bind off next 3 sts in pat, work 12 more sts (13 sts for front), bind off next 3 sts in pat, work 14 sts (14 sts for half back).
With a separate ball of yarn for each section of sts, work each section even in seed st all at once until armholes measure 1½"/4cm, end with a WS row.
Joining inc row (RS) Work seed st across all sts, casting on 1 st only over each set of 3 bound-off sts and closing gaps between sections—43 sts.
Work even in seed st for 1"/2.5cm more, end with a WS row.
Dec row (RS) K1, *k2tog; rep from * to end—22 sts.
Next row Knit.
Cut A.

HEAD
Join B and knit 1 row.
Next row (WS) *K1, p1; rep from * to end.
Rep last row 4 times more for k1, p1 rib.
Next row (RS) *K3, M1; rep from * to last st, k1—29 sts.
Work even in St st (k on RS, p on WS) for 1½"/4cm, end with a WS row.
Dec row 1 (RS) K1, *k2tog; rep from * to end—15 sts.

King Friday the XIII is a loud and boisterous fellow, but his name served a significant purpose. Mister Rogers specifically named him thus to teach children that there is no reason to fear the superstition of bad luck on the day Friday the 13th.

Dec row 2 P1, *p2tog; rep from * to end—8 sts.
Pass last 7 sts over first st one at a time. Fasten off and secure.

SLEEVES
With A and size 8 (5mm) needles, cast on 17 sts. Work even in seed st for 3"/7.5cm. Bind off.

HANDS
First side
With B and size 8 (5mm) needles, make a slipknot and place it on a needle. Knit into front and back of slipknot 3 times—6 sts. Beg with a WS row, work even in St st for 5 rows.
Inc row (RS) Cast on 3 sts, k to end—9 sts.
Purl 1 row.
Dec row Bind off 4 sts, k to end—5 sts.
Work even in St st for ½"/1.5cm. Bind off.

Second side
With B and size 8 (5mm) needles, make a slipknot and place it on a needle. Knit into front and back of slipknot 3 times—6 sts. Beg with a RS row, work even in St st for 5 rows.
Inc row (WS) Cast on 3 sts, p to end—9 sts.
Knit 1 row.
Dec row Bind off 4 sts purlwise, p to end—5 sts.
Work even in St st for ½"/1.5cm. Bind off.

Hold WS of both sides tog and seam around edges.

HAIR
With C and size 8 (5mm) needles, cast on 21 sts.
[Knit 1 row, purl 1 row] twice.
T-twist row (RS) K3, *twist rem sts on LH needle 360 degrees around LH needle, k3; rep from * to end.
Work even in St st for 2"/5cm more, end with a WS row.
Dec row (RS) K1, *k2tog; rep from * to end—11 sts.
Next dec row P1, *p2tog; rep from * to end—6 sts.
Pass last 5 sts over first st one at a time. Fasten off and secure.

BEARD
With C and size 8 (5mm) needles, cast on 15 sts.
[Knit 1 row, purl 1 row] twice.
T-twist row (RS) K3, *twist rem sts on LH needle 360 degrees around LH needle, k3; rep from * to end.
Next row Purl.
Final row (RS) Dec and bind off at same time as foll:
[K2tog] twice, k5, [k2tog] twice, k2.

MUSTACHE
With C and size 8 (5mm) needles, cast on 9 sts.
Knit 1 row, purl 1 row. Bind off.

CROWN
With 2 strands of F held tog and size 4 (3.5mm) needles, cast on 5 sts.
Inc row 1 Sl 1, k1, [yo] twice, k2tog, k1—6 sts.
Row 2 Sl 1, k1, (k1, p1) into double yo, k2.
Inc row 3 Sl 1, k3, [yo] twice, k2—8 sts.
Row 4 Sl 1, k1, (k1, p1) into double yo, k4.
Inc row 5 Sl 1, k1, [yo] twice, k2tog, k4—9 sts.
Row 6 Sl 1, k4, (k1, p1) into double yo, k2.
Row 7 Sl 1, k8
Dec row 8 Bind off 4 sts, k to end—5 sts.
Rep rows 1–8 six times more. Bind off rem 5 sts.
Sew cast-on and bound-off edges tog.
Sew 1 blue bead beneath each of center 5 points of crown.

King Friday the XIII Puppet

CAPE

With C and size 8 (5mm) needles, cast on 53 sts. Knit 2 rows. Cut C. Join D.

Beg with a RS row, work in St st for 4½"/11.5cm, end with a WS row.

Dec row 1 (RS) K12, [S2KP, k10] twice, SK2P, k12—47 sts. Work 3 rows even in St st.

Dec row 2 (RS) K11, [S2KP, k8] twice, SK2P, k11—41 sts. Work 3 rows even in St st.

Dec row 3 (RS) K10, [S2KP, k6] twice, SK2P, k10—35 sts. Work 3 rows even in St st.

Dec row 4 (RS) K9, [S2KP, k4] twice, SK2P, k9—29 sts. Work 3 rows even in St st.

Dec row 5 (RS) K8, [S2KP, k2] twice, SK2P, k8—23 sts.

Collar

Row 1 (WS) Knit.

Row 2 Purl.

Rep last 2 rows for rev St st (p on RS, k on WS) for 1"/2.5cm, end with a RS row.

Dec row (WS) K1, ssk, k to last 3 sts, k2tog, k1—2 sts dec'd.

Next row Purl.

Rep last 2 rows 4 times more—13 sts.

Final row (WS) Dec and bind off at same time as foll: K1, ssk, bind off to last 3 sts, k2tog, k1.

Sew E to each side edge of cape from beg of collar to cast-on edge. Sew fringe trim along top, curved edge of collar. For tassels, cut 8 pieces of fringe trim approx ¼"/.5cm wide and

secure 3 pieces to each side edge along faux fur trim, evenly spaced (see photos).

FINISHING

Sew pearls and flower-shaped buttons to front of gown (see photos).

Arms

Sew sleeve seams. Sew hands into sleeve bottoms.
With pink embroidery floss, use 3 straight sts to create fingers.
Sew sleeves into armholes, taking care that thumbs are turned inwards towards body.
Lightly stuff arms.

Head

Sew back gown and head seams. Stuff head.
Place and secure hair, beard, and mustache to head and face.
With B, embroider nose with a straight st. With black yarn, embroider eyes with a French knot and a straight st. With C, embroider eyebrows with a straight st. (See photos)
Place crown on head and secure in place.

Cape

Attach first row of collar to base of back of neck. Attach chain at each collar side edge, draped along front of body. Sew rem 2 pieces of fringe trim pieces to side edges of collar where chain was attached. ■

❝ *I believe it's a fact of life that what we have is less important than what we make out of what we have.* ❞

Queen Sara Saturday Puppet

DESIGNED BY Nicky Epstein

It is fitting to give Queen Sara Saturday some extra shine, given her loving nature. A strand of sequined yarn is held with the main yarn of her robe. Metallic yarns at the neck and for the crown bring extra glimmer perfect for her Highness.

◼◼◼▭

FINISHED MEASUREMENTS
Height 13¼"/33.5cm

MATERIALS
• 1 3½oz/100g skein (approx 273yd/246m) of Universal Yarn *Uptown DK* (acrylic) each in #102 Lily (A), #125 Silver (B), #119 Limestone (C), and #127 Wither (D) **3**
• 1 .88oz/25g balls (approx 200yd/183m) of Rozetti Yarns *Cotton Gold* (cotton/payette/metallic) in #1091 (E) **1**
• Small quantities of any Metallic Gold (F) and Metallic Silver (H) **2**
• Approx 20"/51cm of Lion Brand *Go For Faux Thick & Quick* in #098 Baked Alaska (G) **7**
• One pair each sizes 4, 6, and 7 (3.5, 4, and 4.5mm) needles, *or size to obtain gauge*
• One pair of small blue eyes
• 13 flatback diamond crystals
• Small amount of polyester stuffing
• 3"/7.5cm length of small gold chain
• ½yd/.5m of gold cord
• Tapestry needle
• Fabric glue
• Pink and black embroidery floss

GAUGE
20 sts and 28 rows to 4"/10cm over St st using A and size 7 (4.5mm) needles.
Take time to check gauge.

NOTE
Before you begin, wind 2 extra small balls each of B and E to be used when working the gown in 3 sections at the same time.

PUPPET
GOWN
With size 7 (4.5mm) needles and 1 strand each of B and E held tog, cast on 61 sts.
Knit 4 rows.
Beg with a RS row, work in St st (k on RS, p on WS) for 6"/15cm, end with a WS row.
Next row (RS) K18 (18 sts for half back), bind off next 3 sts, k18 (19 sts for front), bind off next 3 sts, k17 (18 sts for half back).
With separate balls of B and E for each section of sts, work each section even in St st all at once until armholes measure 1½"/4cm, end with a RS row.
Joining row (WS) With a single ball of yarn, purl across all sts, closing gaps between sections —55 sts.
Dec row 1 (RS) *K2, k2tog; rep from * to last 3 sts, k2tog, k1—41 sts.
Row 2 Purl.
Dec row 3 *K2, k2tog; rep from * to last st, k1—31 sts.
Row 4 Purl.
Dec row 5 *K2, k2tog; rep from * to last 3 sts, k3—24 sts.
Cut B.

NECKLACE
With 1 strand each of E and F held tog, knit 2 rows.
Dec row (WS) *K1, k2tog; rep from * to end—16 sts.
Cut E and F.

NECK
Join C. Knit 1 row, purl 1 row.

HEAD
Row 1 (RS) *K1, kfb; rep from * to end—24 sts.
Row 2 Purl.

Queen Sara Saturday was a thoughtful and patient ruler in the Neighborhood of Make-Believe, quite a contrast to her husband, King Friday the XIII. Mister Rogers shaped her character after his loving wife, Sara Joanne (who went by her middle name), to whom he was married for 50 years.

Row 3 K5, [kfb] 3 times, k8, [kfb] 3 times, k5—30 sts.
Work even in St st for 1¾"/4.5cm, end with a WS row.
Final row (RS) Dec and bind off at same time as foll: *k1,
k2tog; rep from to end and secure rem st.

SLEEVES

With size 7 (4.5mm) needles and 1 strand each of B and E held
tog, cast on 20 sts.
Knit 2 rows.
Beg with a WS row, work even in St st for 3"/7.5cm. Bind off.

HANDS

First side

With size 6 (4mm) needles and C, make a slipknot and place it
on a needle. Knit into front and back of slipknot 3 times—6 sts.
Beg with a WS row, work even in St st for 5 rows.
Inc row (RS) Cast on 3 sts, k to end—9 sts.
Purl 1 row.
Dec row Bind off 4 sts, k to end—5 sts.
Work even in St st for ½"/1.5cm. Bind off.

Second side

With size 6 (4mm) needles and B, make a slipknot and place it
on a needle. Knit into front and back of slipknot 3 times—6 sts.
Beg with a RS row, work even in St st for 5 rows.
Inc row (WS) Cast on 3 sts, p to end—9 sts.
Knit 1 row.
Dec row Bind off 4 sts purlwise, p to end—5 sts.
Work even in St st for ½"/1.5cm. Bind off.

Hold WS of both sides tog and seam around edges.

CAPE

With size 6 (4mm) needle and 1 strand each of E and F held tog,
cast on 70 sts.
Knit 4 rows. Cut E and F. Join A.
Beg with a RS row, work even in St st for 6"/15cm, end with a
WS row.
Dec row 1 (RS) *K2tog, k5; rep from * to end—60 sts.
Work 3 rows even in St st.
Dec row 2 (RS) *K2tog, k4; rep from * to end—50 sts.
Work 3 rows even in St st.
Dec row 3 (RS) *K2tog, k3; rep from * to end—40 sts.
Purl 1 row.
Dec row 4 (RS) *K2tog, k2; rep from * to end—30 sts.
Purl 1 row.
Dec row 5 (RS) *K2tog, k1; rep from * to end—20 sts.
Purl 1 row.

Collar

Row 1 (RS) *K1, M1, k1; rep from * to end—30 sts.

Row 2 *K2, p2; rep from * to last 2 sts, k2.
Row 3 *P2, k2; rep from * to last 2 sts, p2.
Rep last 2 rows until collar measures 2"/5cm long.
Bind off in rib.

Sew a strand of G to each side edge of cape from beg of collar to cast-on edge.
Glue 5 flatback diamond crystals along faux fur trim, evenly spaced, on each side of cape.

HAIR
With size 6 (4mm) needles and D, cast on 43 sts.
Row 1 (RS) K1, *p1, k1; rep from * to end.
Row 2 P1, *k1, p1; rep from * to end.
Rep last 2 rows for k1, p1 rib until pieces measures 1¾"/4.5cm, end with a WS row.
Dec row 1 (RS) *K2tog; rep from * to last st, k1—22 sts.
Dec row 2 *P2tog; rep from * to end—11 sts.
Dec row 3 *K2tog; rep from * to last st, k1—6 sts.
Dec row 4 *P2tog; rep from * to end—3 sts.

Hair buns
Make a bobble on each of the 3 rem sts as foll:
Inc row 1 (RS) Knit into front, back, front, back, and front of same st—5 sts.
Beg with a WS row, work even in St st for 5 rows.
Dec row (RS) K2tog, k1, k2tog—3 sts.
Final dec row P3tog and secure rem st.
Fold each bobble in half and use tail to secure bound-off edge to head, forming the buns.
Sew side edges of each bun tog.

CROWN
With size 4 (3.5mm) needles and 2 strands of F held tog, cast on 5 sts.
Inc row 1 Sl 1, k1, [yo] twice, k2tog, k1—6 sts.
Row 2 Sl 1, k1, (k1, p1) into double yo, k2.
Inc row 3 Sl 1, k3, [yo] twice, k2—8 sts.
Row 4 Sl 1, k1, (k1, p1) into double yo, k4.
Inc row 5 Sl 1, k1, [yo] twice, k2tog, k4—9 sts.
Row 6 Sl 1, k4, (k1, p1) into double yo, k2.
Row 7 Sl 1, k8
Dec row 8 Bind off 4 sts, k to end—5 sts.

Rep rows 1–8 four times more. Bind off rem 5 sts.
Glue 3 flatback diamond crystals under center 3 points of crown.
Sew cast-on and bound-off edges tog.

FINISHING
Arms
Sew side edges of sleeves tog. Sew hands into sleeve bottoms.
With pink embroidery floss, use 3 long sts to create fingers.
Sew sleeves into armholes, taking care that thumbs are turned inwards towards body. Lightly stuff arms.

Head
Sew back gown and head seams. Stuff head.
Sew hair to head, placing buns at top back of head.
Secure eyes to face. With black embroidery floss, use straight sts to embroider outline of eyes and eyebrows. With C, embroider nose with a French knot. With pink embroidery floss, embroider mouth. (See photos)
Secure crown to head, positioning center jewel at front.

Cape
Attach first row of collar to base of neck. Attach chain at each collar side edge, draping along front of body.
Wrap gold cord around waist and knot at front. ◼

"*Real strength has to do with helping others.*"

X the Owl Puppet

DESIGNED BY Nicky Epstein

You'll get a hoot out of making this puppet. The body is a simple and quick construction with the yarn held double and a small section of intarsia at the top back of the head. Eyes, a beak, and feathers in various sizes and colors make this is a fun knit with plenty of engaging details.

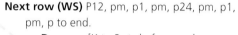

FINISHED MEASUREMENTS
Height 12"/30.5cm

MATERIALS
• 1 3½oz/100g skein (approx 273yd/246m) of Universal Yarn *Uptown DK* each in #115 Lapis (A), #116 Bachelor (B), #102 Lily (C), and #157 Dijon (D) ③
• Small amount of similar weight yarn in Black
• One pair each sizes 6 and 10 (4 and 6mm) needles, *or sizes to obtain gauges*
• Stitch markers
• Small amount of polyester stuffing
• Tapestry needle

Gauges
• 22 sts and 28 rows to 4"/10cm over St st using smaller needles.
• 15 sts and 24 rows to 4"/10cm over St st using 2 strands held tog and larger needles.
Take time to check gauges.

NOTES
1) Before you begin, wind 4 extra small balls of A to be used when working the body in 3 sections at the same time.
2) Chart 2 can be worked from written instructions or chart.
3) The majority of owl is worked with yarn held double. Only the beak and a few of the small feathers use a single strand of yarn.

PUPPET
BODY
With 2 strands of A held tog and larger needles, cast on 51 sts. Knit 4 rows.
Beg with a WS row, work in St st (k on RS, p on WS) for 1½"/4cm, end with a RS row.

Next row (WS) P12, pm, p1, pm, p24, pm, p1, pm, p to end.
Dec row [K to 2 sts before marker, k2tog, sm, k1, sm, ssk] twice, k to end—4 sts dec'd.
Cont in St st and rep dec row on a RS every 1"/2.5cm twice more—39 sts.
Work even in St st until piece measure 5¼"/13.5cm from beg, end with a WS row.
Next dec row (RS) K9 (9 sts for half back), remove markers as you bind off next 3 sts, k15 (16 sts for front), remove markers as you bind off next 3 sts, k to end (9 sts for half back).
Using 2 separate strands of A held tog for each section of sts, work each section even in St st for 5 rows.
Joining row (RS) Using same 2 strands of A held tog, knit across all sts, casting on 2 sts over each set of 3 bound-off sts and closing up gaps—37 sts.
Work even in St st for 3 rows.
Dec row (RS) K6, [k2tog] twice, k to last 10 sts, [k2tog] twice, k6—33 sts.
Purl 1 row.
Dec row [K3, k2tog] 6 times, k3—27 sts.
Purl 1 row.

NECK
Change to smaller needles.
Row 1 (RS) K1, *p1, k1; rep from * to end.
Row 2 P1, *k1, p1; rep from * to end.
Rep last 2 rows until neck measures 1"/2.5cm, end with a WS row.
Change to larger needles. Knit 1 row, purl 1 row.

Mister Rogers was an only child for a good portion of his youth. A quiet and thoughtful boy, he spent many hours playing with puppets by himself. It is no wonder they came so naturally to him as an entertainer and educator.

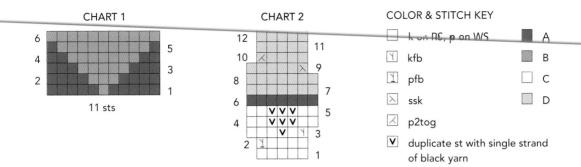

CHART 1

6
5
4
3
2
1

11 sts

CHART 2

12
11
10
9
8
7
6
5
4
3
2
1

COLOR & STITCH KEY

☐	k on RS, p on WS	■	A
⊻	kfb	▨	B
⅄	pfb	☐	C
⊠	ssk	▧	D
⊠	p2tog		
V	duplicate st with single strand of black yarn		

HEAD

Inc row (RS) [K2, kfb, k1, kfb, k2, kfb] 3 times, k2, kfb—37 sts. Work even in St st for 3"/7.5cm, end with a WS row.

Chart 1

Row 1 (RS) K13, pm, work row 1 of chart 1 over next 11 sts, pm, work with A to end.
Cont as established until 6 rows of chart have been worked. Bind off.

ARMS

With larger needles and 2 strands of A held tog, cast on 15 sts. Work even in St st for 2"/5cm, end with a WS row.
Dec row 1 (RS) K1, [k2tog] 7 times—8 sts.
Dec row 2 [P2tog] 4 times—4 sts.
Pass last 3 sts over first st one at a time. Fasten off and secure.

FEATHERS

Large (make 2 with A held double)

With larger needles, cast on 3 sts.
Inc row 1 (RS) Kfb, k1, kfb—5 sts.
Row 2 Purl.
Inc row 3 Kfb, k3, kfb—7 sts.
Rows 4–18 Work even in St st.
Dec row 19 Ssk, k3, k2tog—5 sts.
Row 20 Purl.
Dec row 21 Ssk, k1, k2tog—3 sts.
Row 22 Purl.
Dec row 23 S2KP and secure rem st.

Medium (make 2 with B held double)

With larger needles, cast on 3 sts.
Inc row 1 (RS) Kfb, k1, kfb—5 sts.
Rows 2–12 Work even in St st.
Dec row 13 Ssk, k1, k2tog—3 sts.
Row 14 Purl.
Dec row 15 S2KP and secure rem st.

Small (make 9 with A held double, 6 with B held double, and 5 with 1 strand of B)

With smaller needles, cast on 3 sts.
Inc row 1 (RS) Kfb, k1, kfb—5 sts.
Rows 2–7 Work even in St st.
Dec row 8 Ssk, k1, k2tog—3 sts.
Row 9 Purl.
Row 10 S2KP and secure rem st.

EYES

Note Work eyes with yarn held double throughout.

Center eye circle

With smaller needles and 2 strands of C held tog, cast on 5 sts.
Row 1 (RS) Knit.
Inc row 2 Pfb, p to end—6 sts.
Inc row 3 Kfb, k to end—7 sts.
Row 4 Purl.
Row 5 Knit. Cut both strands of C.
Row 6 Join 2 strands of A. Purl. Cut both strands of A.
Row 7 Join 2 strands of D. Knit.

Row 8 Purl.
Dec row 9 Ssk, k to end—6 sts.
Dec row 10 P2tog, p to end—5 sts.
Row 11 Knit.
Row 12 Purl.
Bind off.
With single strand of black yarn, work duplicate st on center eye (see chart 2).

Outer eye

With 2 strands of B held tog, cast on 26 sts over 2 larger needles held tog. Remove 1 needle from cast-on sts.
Knit 3 rows.
Pass all sts over first st one at a time, AT THE SAME TIME, pull working thread of first st gently to spread sts to form center circle.

Eyelash fringe

With larger needles and 2 strands of B held tog, cast on 7 sts.
*Bind off 6 sts, sl rem st to left hand needle, cast on 5 sts; rep from * 10 times more. Bind off all sts.

BEAK

With smaller needles and single strand of D, cast on 9 sts.
Rows 1 and 2 Work 2 rows even in St st.
Dec row 3 (RS) K3, S2KP, k3—7 sts.
Rows 4–6 Work even in St st.
Dec row 7 K2, S2KP, k2—5 sts.
Rows 8–10 Work even in St st.
Dec row 11 K1, S2KP, k1—3 sts.
Row 12 Purl.
Dec row 13 S2KP and secure rem st.

FINISHING

Sew center back body seam. Sew top of head seam.
Sew cast-on edges of arms into armholes. Seam lengths of arms

Face

Sew center eyes to face. Sew outer eyes in place over center eyes. Sew eyelash fringe to inner edges of outer eyes.
Sew on beak between eyes.
Lightly stuff head.

Feathers

Note See pictures for reference.
Secure 1 small double-strand B feather, 1 small single-strand B

feather, and 1 small A feather at bottom side edge of body.
Rep at opposite side.
Secure 1 large A feather to each shoulder, then secure 1 medium B feather underneath each of those a few sts lower on arm.
Secure 1 small double-strand B feather underneath each medium B feather a few sts lower on arm.
Secure 7 small A feathers across front of neck, then secure 3 small single-strand B feathers above those. ■

"The greatest gift you ever give is your honest self."

Accessories

Making any of these accessories—
that are either replicas of items from
the show or inspired by them—is like
taking a souvenir from the set of
Mister Rogers' Neighborhood.

Colorful Curtains Scarf

DESIGNED BY **Kaffe Fassett**

This scarf is reminiscent of the playful curtains in Mister Rogers' living room. Squares, halved diagonally, are lined up in rows. The bottom half of each row remains the same color so you can carry that strand across the entire row.

FINISHED MEASUREMENTS
Width 14"/35.5cm
Length 67½"/171.5cm

MATERIALS
• 1 1¾oz/50g ball (approx 191yd/175m) of Rowan *Felted Tweed* (wool/viscose/alpaca) each in #153 Phantom (A), #181 Mineral (B), #217 Astor (C), #154 Ginger (D), #213 Lime (E), #212 Peach (F), #184 Celadon (G), #214 Ultramarine (H), #178 Seasalter (I), #216 French Mustard (J), #219 Heliotope (K), #196 Barn Red (L), and #202 Turquoise (M)
• One pair size 6 (4mm) needles, *or size to obtain gauge*
• One size 6 (4mm) circular needle, 40"/100cm or longer

GAUGE
22 sts and 32 rows to 4"/10cm over St st and chart pat using size 6 (4mm) needles.
Take time to check gauge.

NOTES
1) Carry the base color of each row of squares (bottom-right half) across the wrong side of the work. Use a separate length of yarn for each contrasting color (top-left half).
2) Twist yarns on wrong side when changing colors to prevent holes in work.

SCARF
LOWER BORDER
With L and straight needles, cast on 72 sts.
Knit 4 rows. Cut L.
With D, knit 4 rows. Cut D.
With H, knit 4 rows. Cut H.
With I, knit 4 rows. Cut I.

CHART PATTERN
Work chart rows 1–40 a total of 12 times.

UPPER BORDER
With I, knit 4 rows. Cut I.
With H, knit 4 rows. Cut H.
With D, knit 4 rows. Cut D.
With L, knit 4 rows. Bind off knitwise with L.

SIDE BORDERS
With RS facing, circular needle and A, pick up and k 10 sts along side of one border, 7 or 8 sts along side edge of each 10-row stripe, and 10 sts along side of rem border.
Knit 3 rows. Cut A.
Join H and bind off knitwise.
Rep from beg along opposite side border.

FINISHING
Weave in ends. Block to measurements. ■

The curtains in Mister Rogers' home stood out for their colorful and almost chaotic pattern, quite a contrast to his calm, orderly persona and the way he conducted himself. It is noteworthy that his curtains were always open and never shut out his neighbors.

Colorful Curtains Scarf

COLOR & STITCH KEY

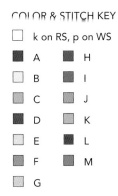

☐ k on RS, p on WS

◼ A   ◼ H
☐ B   ◼ I
◼ C   ◼ J
◼ D   ◼ K
☐ E   ◼ L
◼ F   ◼ M
◼ G

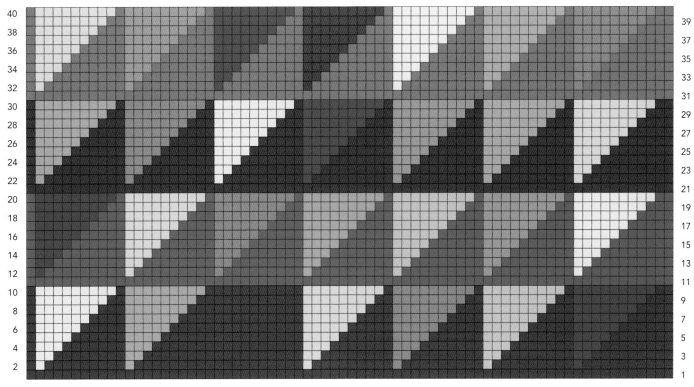

72 sts

"The more I think about it, the more I wonder if
God and neighbor are somehow One. 'Loving God,
Loving neighbor'—the same thing?"

Baby Rogers Sneakers

DESIGNED by Alexandra Davidoff

These little replicas of Mister Rogers' sneakers begin with soles worked in the round. The tongue and sides/back are worked separately in rows. I-cord shoelaces are quickly worked and laced through eyelets.

SIZES
3 months (6 months, 12 months).
Shown in size 3 months.

FINISHED MEASUREMENTS
Sole length 4 (4½, 5)"/10 (11.5, 12.5)cm

MATERIALS
• 1 5oz/140g skein (approx 362yd/331m) of Bernat *Softee Baby* (acrylic) each in #02000 White (A) and #166054 Navy (B) (3)
• One set (5) size 3 (3.25mm) double-pointed needles (dpn), *or size to obtain gauge*
• Stitch marker

GAUGE
26 sts and 32 rows to 4"/10cm over St st using size 3 (3.25mm) needles.
Take time to check gauge.

BOOTIES
SOLE
With A, cast on 28 (32, 40) sts and divide evenly over 4 dpn. Join, take care not to twist sts, pm for beg of rnd (back of shoe).
Rnd 1 Purl.
Inc rnd 2 On Needle 1, k1, M1, k to end; on Needle 2, k to last st, M1, k1; on Needle 3, k1, M1, k to end; on Needle 4, k to last st, M1, k1—4 sts inc'd (1 st inc'd per needle).
Rep last 2 rnds 5 times more—52 (56, 64) sts in total with 13 (14, 16) sts per needle.
Cut A.

TONGUE
Sl first 5 (6, 8) sts of Needle 2 to Needle 1; sl first 8 sts of Needle 3 to Needle 2; sl rem 5 (6, 8) sts

of Needle 3 to Needle 4—18 (20, 24) sts each on Needles 1 and 4, 16 sts on Needle 2. Keeping sts of Needles 1 and 4 on hold, join B with RS facing and work back and forth in rows on Needle 2 as foll:
Row 1 (RS) Knit.
Row 2 Sl 1 wyif, [p2, k1] 5 times.
Row 3 Sl 1 wyif, k to end.
Row 4 Rep row 2.
Dec row 5 Sl 1 wyif, k3, [k2tog, k1] twice, k2tog, k4—13 sts.
Row 6 Sl 1 wyif, p2, [k1, p1] 3 times, k1, p2, k1.
Row 7 Rep row 3.
Row 8 Rep row 6.
Row 9 Rep row 3.
Row 10 Rep row 6.
Dec row 11 Sl 1 wyif, ssk, k to last 3 sts, k2tog, k1—11 sts.
Row 12 Sl 1 wyif, [p1, k1] 5 times.
Row 13 Rep row 3.
Rows 14–21 (14–21, 14–23) Rep rows 12 and 13 four (four, five) times more.
Dec row 22 P2tog, [k1, p1] 3 times, k1, p2tog—9 sts.
Row 23 Ssk, k5, k2tog—7 sts. Bind off.

SIDES AND BACK
With B, work sts of Needles 1 and 4 in rows as foll:
Row 1 (RS) At beg of Needle 4, cast on 6 sts, then beg with

*In 1976, the crew of **Mister Rogers' Neighborhood** decided to play a little prank. When Mister Rogers went to change out of his sneakers and into his outdoor shoes, he found that they were too small for his feet and laughed heartily. Watch this outtake online at misterrogers.org/videos/mister-rogers-puts-on-the-wrong-shoes-outtake.*

the 0 cast on sts, work as foll: k to end of needle 1, cast on 6 sts—48 (52, 60) sts.

Row 2 K2, [p1, k1] twice, p12 (14, 18), [k1, p1] 6 times, p12 (14, 18), [k1, p1] twice, k2.

Rows 3 and 4 Sl 1 wyif, k the knit sts and p the purl sts, making sure to k last st on each row.

Dec eyelet row 5 Sl 1 wyif, p1, k1, yo, k2tog, p1, ssk, k10 (12, 16), [k1, p1] 6 times, k10 (12, 16), k2tog, p1, ssk, yo, k1, p1, k1—46 (50, 58) sts.

Row 6 Sl 1 wyif, k the knit sts and p the yos and purl sts, making sure to k last st.

Dec row 7 Sl 1 wyif, [p1, k1] twice, p1, ssk, k9 (11, 15), [k1, p1] 6 times, k9 (11, 15), k2tog, [p1, k1] 3 times—44 (48, 56) sts.

Row 8 Rep row 6.

Dec eyelet row 9 Sl 1 wyif, p1, k1, yo, k2tog, p1, ssk, k8 (10, 14), [k1, p1] 6 times, k8 (10, 14), k2tog, p1, ssk, yo, k1, p1, k1—42 (46, 54) sts.

Row 10 Rep row 6.

Dec row 11 Sl 1 wyif, [p1, k1] twice, p1, ssk, k7 (9, 13), [k1, p1] 6 times, k7 (9, 13), k2tog, [p1, k1] 3 times—40 (44, 52) sts.

Row 12 Rep row 6.

Dec eyelet row 13 Sl 1 wyif, p1, k1, yo, k2tog, p1, ssk, k6 (8, 12), [ssk] 6 times, k6 (8, 12), k2tog, p1, ssk, yo, k1, p1, k1—32 (36, 44) sts.

Row 14 Rep row 6.

Dec row 15 Sl 1 wyif, [p1, k1] twice, p1, ssk, k to last 8 sts, k2tog, [p1, k1] 3 times—30 (34, 42) sts.

Row 16 Rep row 6.

Rows 17 and 18 (17 and 18, 17–22) Rep row 15 and 16 once (once, 3 times) more—28 (32, 36) sts.
Bind off all sts purlwise.

FINISHING

Weave in ends. Fold sole in half and seam halves of cast-on edge tog with A.
Sew sides of shoe to tongue as foll: with RS facing and B,

overlap sides with tongue, sew tog a bit inwards from the edges so the sides can flap open a bit.

Shoelaces

With A and 2 dpn, cast on 2 sts. Work I-Cord as foll: *Knit one row. Without turning work, slide sts back to opposite end of needle to work next row from RS. Pull yarn tightly from end of row. Rep from * until cord measures 16"/40.5cm, or desired length. Bind off.
Thread shoelaces through eyelet holes. Stitch ends of shoelaces to neaten. ∎

"As different as we are from one another, as unique as each one of us is, we are much more the same than we are different."

Striped Necktie

DESIGNED BY Josh Bennett

Worked in a luxurious alpaca and silk blend over a firm gauge, this knit necktie has a beautiful drape. Knit one for yourself by working garter stitch on the bias and decreasing throughout. The sides are folded during finishing for clean edges.

FINISHED MEASUREMENTS

Width (at widest)
3"/7.5cm
Width (at narrowest)
1½"/4cm
Length (point to point)
55"/140cm

MATERIALS

• 1 1¾oz/50g skein (approx 219yd/200m) of Sandnes Garn *Alpakka Silke* (baby alpaca/ mulberry silk) each in #2135 Ocher (A), #2113 Straw Yellow (B), #2564 Golden Brown (C), and #4035 Dark Terracotta (D) 🧶
• One pair size 3 (3.25mm) needles, *or size to obtain gauge*
• Two size 3 (3.25mm) double-pointed needles (dpn)

GAUGE

28 sts and 48 rows to 4"/10cm over garter st with 2 strands of yarn held tog using size 3 (3.25mm) needles.
Take time to check gauge.

NOTES

1) The necktie is worked with 2 strands of yarn held together throughout.
2) Slip the first stitch and knit last st of every row to create selvage stitches.
3) The necktie is worked on the bias from the wide end to the narrow end.

BIAS PATTERN

Row 1 (RS) Sl 1, kfb, k to last 3 sts, k2tog, k1.
Row 2 Sl 1, k2tog, k to last 2 sts, kfb, k1.
Rep rows 1 and 2 for bias pat.

STRIPE PATTERN

32 rows with 2 strands of A.
20 rows with 1 strand each of A and B.
16 rows with 2 of strands B.
6 rows with 1 strand each of B and C.
6 rows with 2 strands of B.
4 rows with 2 strands of C.
4 rows with 1 strand each of A and C.
6 rows with 2 strands of C.
24 rows with 1 strand each of A and C.
20 rows with 2 strands of C.
6 rows with 1 strand each of B and C.
18 rows with 2 strands of B.
22 rows with 1 strand each of A and B.
68 rows with 2 strands of A.
50 rows with 1 strand each of A and C.
102 rows with 1 strand each of B and C.
60 rows with 2 strands of B.
There are 462 rows in total.

NECKTIE

With 2 strands of A held tog, cast on 45 sts.
Set-up row (WS) Sl 1, k to end.
Foll stripe pat, work bias pat for 60 rows.

While his wardrobe is best known for tennis shoes and cardigans, Mister Rogers wore a necktie more often than not. These were usually in colors more conservative than his bright cardigans.

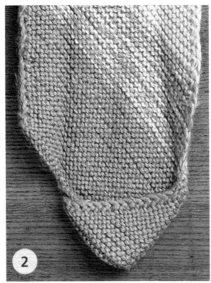

BEGIN DECREASES

Cont stripe pat as foll:

Row 3 (RS) Sl 1, kfb, k to last 3 sts, k2tog, k1.

Dec row 4 (WS) Sl 1, k2tog, k to end—1 st dec'd.

*Work bias pat for 18 rows more.

Rep rows 3 and 4.

Rep from * 16 times more—27 sts.

Work bias pat for 60 rows more.

Bind off.

TAB

With dpn and 2 strands of D, cast on 4 sts. Work I-cord as foll: *Knit 1 row. Without turning work, slide sts back to opposite end of needle to work next row from RS. Pull yarn tightly from end of row. Rep from * until I-cord measures approx 3½"/9cm. Bind off.

FINISHING

Weave in ends. Block lightly.

Lay tie with WS facing up (dec edge on the right and inc edge on the left). Fold first 15 cast-on sts on RH side to match up with next 15 cast-on sts and sew these sts tog along cast-on edge to form point at wide edge.

Fold each outer edge of tie to WS so selvages begin to meet at center back approx 1¾"/4.5cm above folded edge of tie at wider end and stop meeting approx 2½"/6.5cm above point at narrow end. This creates the triangular points at each end (see photos above). Adjust how the edges lay, as necessary, to ensure a smooth dec from first 60 rows to last 60 rows (where dec shaping takes place). Whip st edges tog where they meet.

Steam block edges of tie to help form crease that will maintain the shape.

Fold a tiny portion of each end of tab and sew those folded edges to center of back of tie approx 8½"/21.5cm above point at wide end. ■

> **"***Development comes from within. Nature does not hurry but advances slowly.***"**

Mr. McFeely's Speedy Delivery Hat

DESIGNED BY Linda M. Perry

Worked in pieces, this hat comes together during finishing. The hat itself is felted to provide extra shape and stability. Heavy interfacing gives the brim its structure. Two gold buttons and a covered button on top add special flare.

FINISHED MEASUREMENTS

Brim Circumference 20"/51cm

MATERIALS

- 1 3½oz/100g hank (approx 332yd/304m) of JaggerSpun *Maine Line ⅜ Sport* (wool) in Williamsburg Blue (MC) (**2**)
- 1 1¾oz/50g hank (approx 166yd/152m) of JaggerSpun *Maine Line ⅜ Sport* (wool) each in Black (A) and Natural (B) (**2**)
- One size 5 (3.75mm) circular needle, 16"/40cm long, *or size to obtain gauge*
- One pair size 5 (3.75mm) needles
- One set (5) size 5 (3.75mm) double-pointed needles (dpn)
- Black embroidery thread
- Embroidery needle
- Sewing needle and black thread
- Two ½"/13mm gold buttons
- One ¾"/19mm button
- Interfacing: heavy nonwoven 3 x 9"/7.5 x 23cm
- Eight stitch markers

GAUGE

24 sts and 32 rows to 4"/10cm over St st (before felting) using size 5 (3.75mm) needles.
Take time to check gauge.

NOTES

1) For a firmer ribbing, work corrugated rib with 2 balls of MC. Work in k1, p1 rib, working the knit sts with one ball of MC and the purl sts with a second ball of MC, carrying the two yarns across the wrong side of the work as in Fair Isle knitting.
2) Visor and body of the hat are felted to help retain the shape.
3) See diagrams and create templates from a sturdy cardboard or other material to the specified measurements. You will use these to block your felted pieces.

HAT
BRIM

Roll an extra ball of MC (approx 24yd/22m) and designate it as MC2. Main ball will be MC.

Beg with brim, with circular needle and MC, cast on 128 sts. Join, taking care not to twist sts, and pm for beg of rnd.
Rnd 1 *With MC, k1; with MC2, p1; rep from * around.
Rep rnd 1 for corrugated rib until piece measures 1¾"/4.5cm. Cut MC2 and cont with MC only.
Next rnd Knit.
Inc rnd *K8, M1; rep from * around—144 sts.
Cont in St st (k every rnd) for 1"/2.5cm more.
Inc rnd *K6, M1; rep from * around—168 sts.
Knit 5 rnds, placing a marker every 21 sts on final rnd (8 sections).

SHAPE TOP

Note Change to dpn when sts no longer fit comfortably on circular needle.
Dec rnd 1 [K to 3 sts before marker, S2KP, sm] 8 times—16 sts dec'd.
Rnd 2 Knit.
Rep last 2 rnds 5 times more—72 sts.
Knit 3 rnds.
Rep dec rnd 1.
Rep last 4 rnds twice more—24 sts.
Knit 1 rnd.
Next dec rnd *K1, k2tog; rep from * around—16 sts.
Knit 2 rnds.
Next dec rnd *K2tog; rep from * around—8 sts.
Cut yarn, leaving a 6"/15cm tail. With tapestry needle, thread yarn through rem sts and pull tightly. Secure. Weave in ends.

VISOR

With straight needles and A, cast on 100 sts. Knit 1 row. Divide sts evenly over 4 dpn (25 sts per needle). Join, taking care not to twist sts, and pm for beg of rnd.
Rnds 1–10 Knit.
Dec rnd 11 K2tog, k46, k2tog, pm, k2tog, k46, k2tog—96 sts.
Dec rnd 12 [K2tog, k to 2 sts before marker, k2tog, sm] twice—4 sts dec'd.
Rep dec rnd 12 four times more—76 sts.

Like others, the character Mr. McFeely was drawn from Mister Rogers' personal life. His maternal grandfather, Fred McFeely, was a direct inspiration for the delivery man we meet time and again on Mister Rogers' Neighborhood.

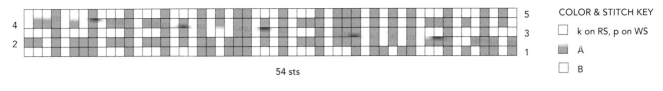

54 sts

COLOR & STITCH KEY

☐ k on RS, p on WS

▨ A

☐ B

Transfer half the sts to one straight needle and other half to other straight needle. Bind off using 3-needle bind-off (see page 125).

SPEEDY DELIVERY BAND

With A, cast on 60 sts.
Knit 1 row, purl 1 row.

Chart

Inc row 1 (RS) K1, M1, k2, pm, work row 1 of chart over 54 sts, pm, k2, M1, k1—2 sts inc'd.

Inc row 2 P1, M1P, p to marker, sm, work next row of chart, sm, p to last st, M1P, p1—2 sts inc'd.

Inc row 3 K1, M1, k to marker, sm, work next row of chart, sm, k to last st, M1, k1—2 sts inc'd.

Rep last 2 rows twice more, working all sts in A when chart is complete—74 sts.

Bind off knitwise on WS.

Weave in ends. Steam block.

FINISHING
Felt hat and visor

Immerse hat and visor only (not speedy delivery band) in hot soapy water, followed by cold water, and rub. Rep until sts begin to felt. Rinse and remove excess water.

Place each piece on its prepared template (see note 3). Allow to fully dry.

If desired, lightly steam block to further smooth shapes.

Top button

With MC, knit a swatch approx 1¼"/3cm square. Felt as for hat and visor. Wrap around button and sew edges of swatch to secure in place.

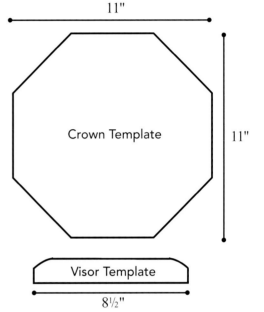

11"

11"

Crown Template

Visor Template

8½"

Assembly

Sew speedy delivery band to brim of hat, leaving bottom edge open.

Place cut interfacing in visor. Sew open edges tog with ½"/1cm interfacing not covered. Sew through two layers of knitted fabric and interfacing to close seam. This reinforcement will allow visor to maintain an L shape as it sticks out of brim. Notch exposed interfacing 5–6 times along its length. Insert exposed interfacing between speedy delivery band and brim of hat, sew in place. Sew underneath edge of visor to brim so all knitted areas are butted together. Sew gold buttons to each top outer corner of speedy delivery band and covered button to center top of cap. ■

> "*Some days, doing 'the best we can' may still fall short of what we would like to be able to do, but life isn't perfect—on any front—and doing what we can with what we have is the most we should expect of ourselves or anyone else.*"

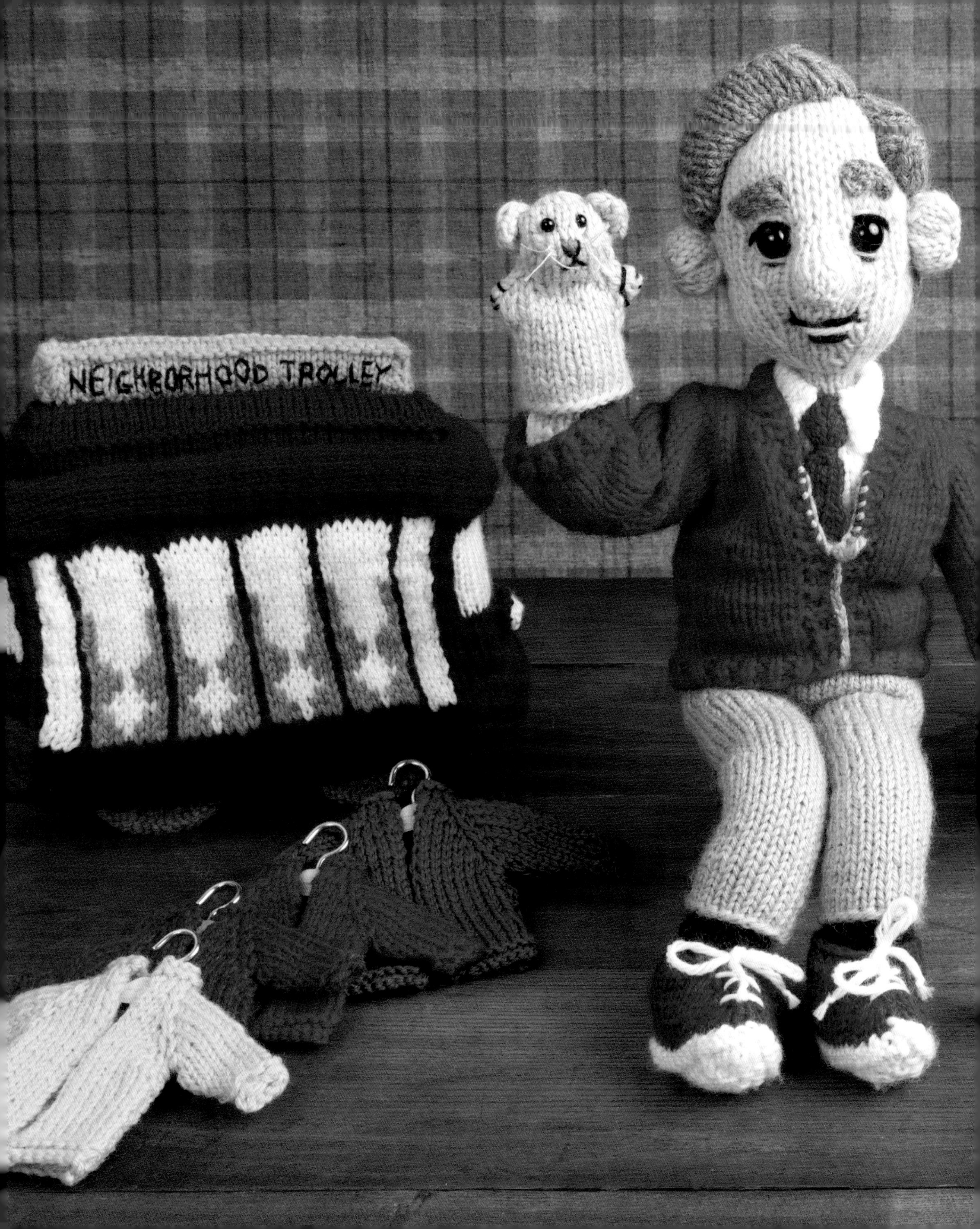
NEIGHBORHOOD TROLLEY

Toys

Knit up fish, mini-cardigans, a Neighborhood Trolley, or even a little Mister Rogers doll (that you can make posable by inserting wire along with the stuffing). These toys are so lovable and squishable that everyone—adult and kids alike—will want one.

Neighborhood Trolley

DESIGNED BY Megan Kreiner

Travel to the Neighborhood of Make-Believe with this detailed knit version of the neighborhood trolley. Start with the base before knitting each side separately. The roof and signboard, bumpers, lights, and wheels are worked separately and then assembled together.

◀■■▢

FINISHED MEASUREMENTS
Height 7½"/16cm
Width 8½"/21.5cm
Depth 4"/10cm

MATERIALS
- 1 3½oz/100g hank (approx 220yd/200m) of Cascade Yarns *Cascade 220* (Peruvian highland wool) each in #8555 Black (A), #2413 Red (B), #8505 White (C), #7826 California Poppy (D), #9564 Birch Heather (E), and #9463B Gold (F) (**4**)
- One set (5) size 4 (3.5mm) double-pointed needles (dpn)
- Removable stitch markers
- Four stitch holders
- Foam stabilizer
- 1"/2.5cm thick cushion foam
- Polyester stuffing
- Black embroidery floss
- Tapestry needle
- Marking pins

GAUGE
24 sts and 34 rnds to 4"/10cm over St st using size 4 (3.5mm) needles. *Gauge is not vital for this project, but it is best to keep stitches tight to keep stuffing from showing through.*

NOTE
Work charts in Stockinette stitch using a separate strand of yarn for each color section. Twist yarns on WS to prevent holes in work. If desired, center red columns on Long Side chart can be worked in duplicate stitch.

STITCH GLOSSARY
M1R Insert LH needle from back to front under strand between last st worked and next st on LH needle, k into front loop to twist st—1 st inc'd.
M1L Insert LH needle from front to back under strand between last st worked and next st on LH needle, k into back loop to twist st—1 st inc'd.

NEIGHBORHOOD TROLLEY
BASE
With A, cast in 60 sts and divide evenly over 4 dpn. Join, taking care not to twist sts, and pm for beg of rnd.
Inc rnd 1 [Kfb, M1R, k28, M1L, kfb] twice—68 sts.
Rnds 2, 4, 6, 8, 10, 12, and 14 Knit.
Inc rnd 3 [K1, kfb, M1R, k30, M1L, kfb, k1] twice—76 sts.
Inc rnd 5 [K2, kfb, M1R, k32, M1L, kfb, k2] twice—84 sts.
Inc rnd 7 [K3, kfb, M1R, k34, M1L, kfb, k3] twice—92 sts.
Inc rnd 9 [K4, kfb, M1R, k36, M1L, kfb, k4] twice—100 sts.
Inc rnd 11 [K5, kfb, M1R, k38, M1L, kfb, k5] twice—108 sts.
Inc rnd 13 [K6, kfb, M1R, k40, M1L, kfb, k6] twice—116 sts.
Inc rnd 15 [K7, kfb, M1R, k42, M1L, kfb, k7] twice—124 sts.
Rnds 16 and 17 Purl.
Rnds 18–20 Knit.
Rnd 21 P9, pm, p44, pm, p18, pm, p44, pm, p9. Cut yarn.
Place sts on 4 holders, dividing as foll: first 9 sts and last 9 sts of rnd for 18 sts for first short side, next 44 sts for first long side, next 18 sts for 2nd short side, and rem 44 sts for 2nd long side. Seam halves of cast-on edge tog using mattress st.

LONG SIDES
Place one set of 44 sts on needle. Join B, ready to work RS.
Dec row 1 (RS) K21, SKP, k21—43 sts.
Beg with row 2 of Long Side chart, work through row 23, keeping floats loose. With B, bind off purlwise on WS.
Rep for 2nd long side.

SHORT SIDES
Place one set of 18 sts on needle. Join B, ready to work RS. Beg with row 1 of Short Side chart, work through row 23, keeping floats loose. With B, bind off purlwise on WS.
Rep for 2nd short side.

Block pieces to help relax floats and flatten panels. Match up and sew side edges tog.

One of the most iconic features of Mister Rogers' Neighborhood is the neighborhood trolley that traveled from Mister Rogers' home to the Neighborhood of Make-Believe. Every year, it traveled approximately 5,000 miles on set!

NEIGHBORHOOD TROLLEY

DUMPERS

With B, cast on 48 sts and divide evenly over 4 dpn. Join, taking care not to twist sts, and pm for beg of rnd.

Rnd 1 Knit.

Rnds 2 and 3 P24, k24.

Rnds 4–6 Knit.

Rnds 7 and 8 P24, k24.

Rnd 9 Knit.

Divide sts evenly over 2 dpn and join using Kitchener stitch (see page 126).

Cut piece of ¾ x 4"/2 x 10cm stabilizer foam to fit and place inside bumper. Seam halves of cast-on edge tog using mattress st. Rep for 2nd bumper.

LIGHTS

With B, cast on 12 sts and divide evenly over 3 dpn. Join, taking care not to twist sts, and pm for beg of rnd.

Rnds 1 and 2 Knit.

Rnd 3 Purl.

Cut B. Join C.

Rnd 4 Knit.

Dec rnd 5 [K2tog] 6 times.

Cut yarn and weave through rem 6 sts. Pull tightly to close hole. Rep for 2nd light.

ROOF

With B, cast on 40 sts and divide evenly over 4 dpn. Join, taking care not to twist sts, and pm for beg of rnd.

Rnd 1 Knit.

Inc rnd 2 K20, k3, M1R, k3, M1R, k8, M1L, k3, M1L, k3—44 sts.

Rnd 3 Knit.

Inc rnd 4 K20, k4, M1R, k4, M1R, k8, M1L, k4, M1L, k4—48 sts.

Rnds 5–63 Knit.

Dec rnd 64 K20, k3, k2tog, k3, k2tog, k8, ssk, k3, ssk, k3—44 sts.

Rnd 65 Knit.

Dec rnd 66 K20, k2, k2tog, k2, k2tog, k4, pm, k4, ssk, k2, ssk, k2—40 sts.

Rnd 67 Knit.

Bind off and cut yarn, leaving a long tail for sewing.

WIth rnd 66 at top of roof, insert a 3 x 7.5"/7.5 x 19cm piece of foam stabilizer into roof. Insert a small amount of stuffing on top of foam so roof slightly domes upward.

Seam closed each open end of roof.

SIGNBOARD

Base

With B, cast on 60 sts and divide evenly over 4 dpn. Join, taking care not to twist sts, and pm for beg of rnd.

Inc rnd 1 [Kfb, M1R, k28, M1L, kfb] twice—68 sts.

Rnd 2 Knit.

Inc rnd 3 [K1, kfb, M1R, k30, M1L, kfb, k1] twice—76 sts.

Rnd 4 Knit.

Inc rnd 5 [K2, kfb, M1R, k32, M1L, kfb, k2] twice—84 sts.

Rnd 6 Knit.

Rnd 7 P4, pm, p34, pm, p8, pm, p34, pm, p4. Cut yarn.

Place sts on 4 holders, dividing as foll: first 4 sts and last 4 sts of rnd for 8 sts for first short side, next 34 sts for first long side, next 8 sts for 2nd short side, and rem 34 sts for 2nd short side.

Long sides

Place one set of 34 sts for a long side on a needle. Join B, ready to work a RS.

Row 1 (RS) Knit.

Row 2 Purl.

Rows 3 and 4 Knit.

Rows 5–10 Work even in St st (k on RS, p on WS).

Place sts on holder.

Rep for 2nd long side.

Place each set of 34 sts on a separate needle and join using Kitchener stitch.

Short sides

Place a set of 8 sts on a needle. Join B, ready to work a RS.

Row 1 (RS) Knit.

Row 2 Purl.

Rows 3 and 4 Knit.

Inc row 5 Kfb, M1R, k6, M1L, kfb—12 sts.

Row 6 Purl.

Dec row 7 K1, [k2tog] twice, k2, [ssk] twice, k1—8 sts.

SHORT SIDE

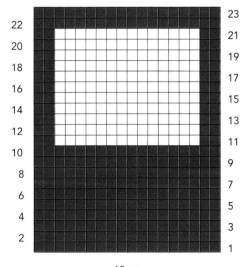

18 sts

Bind off all sts purlwise. Cut yarn, leaving a 12"/30.5cm tail for sewing.
Cut a 1½ x 5½"/3.5 x 14cm cushion foam to fit inside signboard base. Seam bound-off edges of short side to top of base (side edges of long sides), matching purl rows.

Seam halves of cast-on edge tog.

Signage

With F, cast on 36 sts.
Row 1 (RS) K2, p1, k30, p1, k2.
Row 2 P2, k1, p30, k1, p2.
Rows 3–6 Rep rows 1 and 2 twice more.
Row 7 Bind off 3 sts, p to last 3 sts, bind off last 3 sts and cut yarn—30 sts.
Row 8 (WS) Rejoin yarn and purl.
Rows 9–11 Knit.
Rows 12–15 Work even in St st.
Bind off purlwise. Cut yarn, leaving a long tail for sewing.
Fold flaps on edges of rows 1–6 in and sew edge of flaps to edges of rows 11–15 to create a long, narrow box shape.
Cut four 4¾ x ¾"/12 x 2cm pieces of foam stabilizer and insert.
Sew up any rem small holes at ends of sign.

WHEELS

With E, cast on 8 sts and divide evenly over 4 dpn. Join, taking care not to twist sts, and pm for beg of rnd.
Inc rnd 1 [Kfb] 8 times—16 sts.
Rnd 2 Knit.
Inc rnd 3 *K1, M1, k1; rep from * around—24 sts.
Rnd 4 Knit.

Inc rnd 5 *K2, M1, k1; rep from * around—32 sts.
Rnd 6 Purl.
Bind off purlwise and cut yarn, leaving a long tail for sewing.
Fold wheel in half to form semi-circle and sew curved edges tog.
Rep 3 times more for rem wheels.

FINISHING
Trolley car
Cut four 3 x 6¼"/7.5 x 16cm pieces of cushion foam and insert into trolley car. Cut two 3 x 3½"/7.5 x 9cm pieces of stabilizer

COLOR & SITCH KEY

- ☐ k on RS, p on WS
- ☒ SKP
- ■ B
- ☐ C
- ☐ F

LONG SIDE

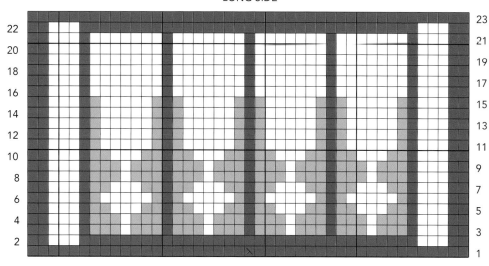

43 sts

foam and place at short ends of trolley car to cover edges of cushion foam.

Place roof on top of trolley car. Seam in place, allowing 2 or 3 sts of overhang along edges. Sew short ends of roof to short ends of trolley car first. Pin long edges of trolley car evenly along bottom edges of roof before sewing to help keep seat and post details straight.

Bumpers

With purl st details facing out and whip-stitch seam at bottom, wrap bumpers over short ends of trolley, covering black portion of base so short sides of bumper align with first column of C sts on short sides. Secure bumper to trolley with upper edge aligned with first row of color B on sides.

Window Frames

On short sides of car, use B to draw a series of running sts underneath columns of B sts that border windows, pulling gently to puff out columns.

Lights

Stuff lightly. Sew open edges of lights to short sides of trolley centered between bumpers and windows.

Sign Base

Place sign base on top of roof with Kitchener seam facing up. Secure short ends and then long ends in place.

Shape roof with a very loose running st placed between seam of roof and sign base. This will help reduce overall puffiness and to help further define roof overhang.

Signage

Place open edge of signage on top of sign base. Sew in place with F.
With marking pins, mark placement for 12 letters of NEIGHBORHOOD, 1 space, and 7 letters of TROLLEY. With black embroidery floss, stitch on letters.
Rep on other side.

Wheels

Place flat edges of semicircle wheels against bottom of trolley car, half-way between middle and short edges of the car. Secure in place. ∎

"*You can think about things and make believe. All you have to do is think and they'll grow.***"**

Fish and Food Shaker

DESIGNED BY Megan Kreiner

Knit a fish—or an entire school—by working the body flat with intarsia. Then, seam and stuff the body before adding cute eyes and fins. Don't forget the food shaker, worked quickly in the round, to keep those fish bellies full and happy.

◼◼◼▭

Finished Measurements

FISH
Length 4½"/11.5cm
Height 2"/5cm
Width 3½"/9cm
FOOD SHAKER
Height 4½"/11.5cm
Width 2½"/6.5cm

MATERIALS

• 1 3½oz/100g skein (approx 220yd/200m) of Cascade Yarns *Cascade 220* (Peruvian highland wool) each in #9605 Tiger Lily (A), #1037 Faded Denim (B), #8836 Stonewash (C), #8505 White (D), #9669 Gold Fusion (E), #9542 Blaze (F), and #2414 Ginger (G) 🧶
• Small quantity of black yarn
• One pair size 4 (3.5mm) needles, *or size to obtain gauge*
• One set (5) size 4 (3.5 mm) double-pointed needles (dpn)
• Stitch markers
• Foam stabilizer
• 1"/2.5cm thick cushion foam
• Small amount of polyester stuffing
• Tapestry needle
• One pair of ½"/12mm plastic safety eyes per fish

Gauge

24 sts and 34 rows/rnds to 4"/10 cm over St st using size 4 (3.5 mm) needles.
Gauge is not vital for this project, but it is best to keep stitches tight to keep stuffing from showing through.

NOTE

1) For fish, work each section of color with a separate ball. Twist yarns on WS to prevent holes in work.
2) Choose your MC and CC before starting each fish.

STITCH GLOSSARY

M1R Insert LH needle from back to front under strand between last st worked and next st on LH needle, k into front loop to twist st—1 st inc'd.
M1L Insert LH needle from front to back under strand between last st worked and next st on LH needle, k into back loop to twist st—1 st inc'd.

FISH
BODY

With MC, cast on 9 sts.
Row 1 (WS) Purl.
Inc row 2 [Kfb, k1, kfb] 3 times —15 sts.
Row 3 Purl.
Inc row 4 With MC, k1, M1R, k3, M1L, k1; with CC, k1, M1R, k3, M1L, k1; with MC, k1, M1R, k3, M1L, k1—21 sts.
Row 5 With MC, p7; with CC, p7; with MC, p7.
Row 6 With MC, k7; with CC, k7; with MC, k7.
Row 7 Rep row 5.
Inc row 8 With MC, k2, M1R, k3, M1L, k2; with CC, k2, M1R, k3, M1L, k2; with MC, k2, M1R, k3, M1L, k2—27 sts.
Rows 9–17 Work even in St st (k on RS, p on WS), matching colors.
Dec row 18 With MC, k1, k2tog, k3, ssk, k1; with CC, k1, k2tog, k3, ssk, k1; with MC, k1, k2tog, k3, ssk, k1—21 sts.
Rows 19 and 21 Rep row 5.
Row 20 Rep row 6.
Dec row 22 With MC, k1, k2tog, k1, ssk, k1; with CC, k1, k2tog, k1, ssk, k1; with MC, k1, k2tog, k1, ssk, k1—15 sts.
Row 23 With MC, p5; with CC, p5; with MC, p5.
Row 24 With MC, k5; with CC, k5; with MC, k5.
Row 25 Rep row 23.
Dec row 26 With MC, k2tog, k1, ssk; with CC, k2tog, k1, ssk; with MC, k2tog, k1, ssk—9 sts.

Mister Rogers often took time to feed the fish in his fish tank during his show. Whenever he did, he would announce it. This was because a blind viewer once asked him to do so so that she would know the fish were okay.

Row 27 With MC, p3; with CC, p3; with MC, p3.
Cut CC. Cont with MC only.
Row 28 Knit.
Row 29 Purl.
Dec rnd 30 K1, k2tog, k3, ssk, k1—7 sts.
Bind off purlwise, leaving a long tail for seaming.
With tail from bind-off, sew back seam, leaving a 1"/2.5cm opening. Stuff body.
Attach safety eyes on either side of body (see photo). If not adding safety eyes, use black yarn to embroider eyes using satin st or French knots.
Add more stuffing, if needed, and close seam, leaving cast-on edge open in a small circle. Apply a running st through 2nd row of body and pull gently to pucker mouth.
Apply a few small satin stitches of E to inside of mouth to help define it.

TAIL FINS

With MC, cast on 3 sts, leaving a long tail for sewing.
Inc row 1 Kfb, k1, kfb—5 sts.
Row 2 [P1, k1] twice, p1.
Inc row 3 Kfb, p1, k1, p1, kfb—7 sts.
Row 4 [K1, p1] 3 times, k1.
Row 5 [P1, k1] 3 times, p1.
Row 6 Rep row 4.
Bind-off row [Cast on 2 sts, k the 2 sts just cast on, on RH needle pass 2nd st over first st to bind off 1 st, p1, bind off 1 st, k1, bind off 1 st, p1, bind off 1 st, wyib sl last st from right to left needle] 3 times, fasten off last st.
Rep for 2nd fin.
Attach cast-on rows of tail fins to back end of body, vertically positioned, stacked one on top of the other. Weave in ends.

SIDE AND BACK FINS

With MC, cast on 3 sts, leaving a long tail for sewing.
Work rows 1–4 same as tail fin—7 sts.
Work bind-off row same as tail fin.
Rep to make 2 more fins.
For side fins, pinch and sew corners of cast-on edge tog, then attach to opposite sides of body.
For back fin, attach cast-on edge to top center of back.
Weave in ends.

FISH FOOD SHAKER

With E, cast on 5 sts and divide over 4 dpn. Join, taking care not to twist sts, and pm for beg of rnd.
Inc rnd 1 [Kfb] 5 times—10 sts.
Rnd 2 Knit.
Inc rnd 3 [K1, M1R] 10 times—20 sts.
Rnd 4 Knit.
Inc rnd 5 [K1, M1R, k1] 10 times—30 sts.
Rnd 6 Knit.
Inc rnd 7 [K1, M1R, k2] 10 times—40 sts.
Rnd 8 Knit.
Rnds 9 and 10 Purl.
Cut E. Join F.
Rnds 11–36 Knit.
Cut F. Join E.
Rnd 37 Knit.
Rnds 38 and 39 Purl.
Cut E. Join G.
Rnds 40–45 Knit.

Cut two 1¾"/4.5cm circles of cushion foam and cut one 3¾ x 6½"/9.5 x 16.5cm rectangle of foam stabilizer.
Make shorter sides of foam stabilizer meet to form a tube and then insert it into the shaker so it lines the walls.
Place 1 cushion foam circle at bottom of shaker, inside foam lining. Add stuffing.
Place 2nd cushion foam circle inside the foam lining on top of stuffing. The foam and stuffing should reach rnd 40 of shaker.

Dec rnd 46 [K1, ssk, k1] 10 times—30 sts.
Rnd 47 Knit.
Dec rnd 48 [K1, ssk] 10 times—20 sts.
Rnd 49 Knit.
Dec rnd 50 [Ssk] 10 times—10 sts.
Rnd 51 Knit.

Cut four 2¼"/5.5cm foam stabilizer circles and insert into opening to shape top of shaker.
Cut yarn, thread through rem sts, and pull to close.
Weave in ends.
With black yarn, embroider short sts to top of shaker. ∎

"There are three ways to ultimate success: The first way is to be kind. The second way is to be kind. The third way is to be kind."

Mini Mister Rogers Doll

DESIGNED BY Megan Kreiner

This knitted Mister Rogers doll is eager to be your neighbor. You can change his penny loafers with sneakers and have him play with the mini version of Daniel Striped Tiger. For extra posability, add paper-wrapped floral wire to the body during assembly.

◼◼◼◼

FINISHED MEASUREMENTS
Height 14"/35.5cm
Width 4"/10cm

Materials
• 1 3½oz/100g skein (approx 220yd/200m) of Cascade Yarns *Cascade 220* (Peruvian highland wool) each in #1033 Nectarine (A), #8555 Black (B), #8393 Navy (C), #9499 Sand (D), #8505 White (E), #7818 Blue Velvet (F), #8895 Christmas Red (G), #2414 Ginger (H), #8509 Grey (I), #8021 Beige (J), and #1009 Storm Cloud (K) ▨
• One set (5) size 4 (3.5mm) double-pointed needles, *or size to obtain gauge*
• One pair size 4 (3.5 mm) needles
• Removable stitch markers
• Stitch holders
• Polyester stuffing
• Paper-wrapped floral wire, optional
• One pair ½"/12mm safety eyes
• One pair 4mm safety eyes
• Black, dark pink, and gold embroidery thread
• White thread
• Tapestry needle
• Marking pins

GAUGE
24 sts and 34 rnds to 4"/10 cm over St st using size 4 (3.5 mm) needles.
Gauge is not vital for this project, but it is best to keep stitches tight to keep stuffing from showing through.

NOTE
Rather than using safety eyes, you can embroider them instead.

STITCH GLOSSARY
M1R Insert LH needle from back to front under strand between last st worked and next st on LH needle, k into front loop to twist st—1 st inc'd.

M1L Insert LH needle from front to back under strand between last st worked and next st on LH needle, k into back loop to twist st—1 st inc'd.

DOLL
HEAD
With A, cast on 8 sts and divide evenly over 4 dpn. Join, taking care not to twist sts, and pm for beg of rnd.
Inc rnd 1 [Kfb] 8 times—16 sts.
Rnd 2 Knit.
Inc rnd 3 [K1, M1R, k6, M1L, k1] twice—20 sts.
Rnd 4 Knit.
Inc rnd 5 [(K1, M1R) 3 times, k4, (M1L, k1) 3 times] twice —32 sts.
Rnd 6 Knit.
Inc rnd 7 [(K1, M1R, k1) twice, k8, (k1, M1L, k1) twice] twice—40 sts.
Rnds 8–16 Knit.
Note On marker rnds, place markers on sts and leave in place.
Ear marker dec rnd 17 [K1, pm, k2tog, k2, k2tog, K5, (k1, ssk, k1) twice] twice—32 sts.
Nose marker rnd 18 K8, pm, k24.
Rnds 19–22 Knit.
Ear marker dec rnd 23 [K1, pm, k2tog, k1, k2tog, k4, (ssk, k1) twice] twice—24 sts.
Rnd 24 Knit.
Inc rnd 25 [(K1, M1R) twice, k8, (M1L, k1) twice] twice —32 sts.
Rnd 26 Knit.

Mister Rogers led a full life with many achievements. He was a high school student president, earned a Bachelor of Music degree, became an ordained minister, was inducted into the Television Hall of Fame, and received more than 40 honorary degrees.

Inc rnd 27 [K1, M1R, k14, M1L, k1] twice—36 sts.
Rnds 28–30 Knit.
Dec rnd 31 [(K1, k2tog, k1) twice, k2, (k1, ssk, k1) twice] twice—28 sts.
Rnd 32 Knit.
Dec rnd 33 [(K1, k2tog,) twice, k2, (ssk, k1) twice] twice—20 sts.
Rnd 34 Knit.
Dec rnd 35 [K1, k2tog, k4, ssk, k1] twice—16 sts.
Rnd 36 Knit.
Stuff head.
Cut yarn and weave tail through rem 16 sts. Do not pull shut.

Ears
With A, cast on 8 sts and divide evenly over 4 dpn. Join, taking care not to twist sts, and pm for beg of rnd.
Inc rnd 1 [Kfb] 8 times—16 sts.
Rnds 2–5 Knit.
Dec rnd 6 [K1, k2tog, k2, ssk, k1] twice—12 sts.
Bind off.
Fold piece in half and sew halves of bound-off edge tog with whip st. Sew halves of cast-on edge tog with mattress st.
Attach bound-off edge to side of head between ear markers on rnds 17 and 23.
Rep for 2nd ear, attaching to opposite side of head. Remove ear markers.

Nose
With A, cast on 10 sts and divide over 3 dpn. Join, taking care not to twist sts, and pm for beg of rnd.
Rnd 1 Knit.
Inc rnd 2 [K1, M1R, k3, M1L, k1] twice—14 sts.
Rnd 3 Knit.
Dec rnd 4 [K1, k2tog, k1, ssk, k1] twice—10 sts.
Rnd 5 Knit.
Note On next rnd, place removable marker on st and leave in place. This marks the side you will attach to the face.
Dec rnd 6 K2tog, k1, pm, ssk, k5—8 sts.
Rnds 7 and 8 Knit.
Dec rnd 9 K3, k2tog, k1, ssk—6 sts.
Stuff nose lightly.
Cut yarn, thread tail through rem 6 sts, and pull firmly to close. Seam cast on edge with whip st.
Place bottom of nose at nose marker on head, between ears. Remove markers on face and nose. Sew top of nose bridge and sides of nose to face.

Attach 12mm safety eyes on either side of nose. Using A, run yarn back and forth through head between inner corners of eyes 2–3 times, pulling gently to shape nose bridge and sink eyes into head.

Eyebrows
With K, cast on 7 sts, Bind off.
Rep for 2nd eyebrow.

Position eyebrows above eyes. If one end looks thicker, position thicker end towards center of face. With K, secure in place.

Hair
Back
Note On marker rnds, place markers on sts and leave in place.
With K, cast on 8 sts and divide evenly over 4 dpn. Join, taking care not to twist sts, and pm for beg of rnd.
Inc rnd 1 [Kfb] 8 times—16 sts.
Rnd 2 Knit.
Inc rnd 3 [(K1, M1R) twice, k4, (M1L, k1) twice] twice—24 sts.

Rnd 4 Knit.
Inc rnd 5 [(K1, M1R) 3 times, k6, (M1L, k1) 3 times] twice—36 sts.
Rnd 6 Knit.
Inc rnd 7 [(K1, M1R, k2) 3 times, (k2, M1L, k1) 3 times] twice—48 sts.
Rnds 8–12 Knit.
Dec rnd 13 [K1, (k2tog) twice, k14, (ssk) twice, k1] twice—40 sts.
Rnds 14–15 Knit.

Hair marker inc rnd 16 K1, pm, k20, pm, k19.

Rnds 17–18 Knit.

Inc rnd 19 [(K1, M1R, k2) 3 times, k2, (k2, M1L, k1) 3 times] twice—52 sts.

Rnds 20–24 Knit.

Dec rnd 25 [(K1, k2tog, k1) 3 times, k2, (k1, ssk, k1) 3 times] twice—40 sts.

Rnd 26 Knit.

Dec rnd 27 [(K1, k2tog) 3 times, k2, (ssk, k1) 3 times] twice—28 sts.

Rnd 28 Knit.

Dec rnd 29 [(K1, k2tog) twice, k2, (ssk, k1) twice] twice—20 sts.

Rnd 30 Knit.

Dec rnd 31 [K1, (k2tog) twice, (ssk) twice, k1] twice—12 sts.

Place first half of sts on a dpn and 2nd half of sts on another dpn. With RS held tog, bind off using 3-needle bind-off (see page 125).

Turn piece RS out. Seam cast-on edge tog with whip st. Flatten and align rnd 31 of with top of head, positioning rnd 16 markers directly behind ears. Secure edges to head with a running st.

Right Front

With K, cast on 40 sts and divide evenly over 2 dpn. Join, taking care not to twist sts, and pm for beg of rnd.

Rnds 1–4 Knit.

Dec rnd 5 K1, [k2tog] twice, k12, ssk, k2, k2tog, k12, [ssk] twice, k1—34 sts.

Rnd 6 Knit.

Dec rnd 7 K1, pm, [k2tog] twice, k24, [ssk] twice, k1—30 sts.

Dec rnd 8 K12, ssk, k2, k2tog, k12—28 sts.

Divide sts evenly over 2 needles, hold parallel, and join with Kitchener st (see page 126). Add a small amount of stuffing. Flatten and whip st cast-on edge closed.

Left Front

With K, cast on 20 sts and divide evenly over 2 dpn. Join, taking care not to twist sts, and pm for beg of rnd.

Rnds 1–3 Knit.

Dec rnd 4 [K1, k2tog, k4, ssk, k1] twice—16 sts.

Rnd 5 Knit.

Dec rnd 6 K1, pm, [k2tog] twice, ssk, k2, k2tog, [ssk] twice, k1—10 sts.

Rnd 7 K2, ssk, k2, k2tog, k2—8 sts.

Divide sts evenly over 2 needles, hold parallel, and join with Kitchener st. Add a small amount of stuffing. Flatten and whip st cast-on edge closed.

Pin cast-on edges of left front and right fronts of hair to top and sides of head directly against front edge of hair back piece. Markers on rnds 6 and 7 of left front and right front of hair should be positioned where the two hair fronts meet slightly off center above face to create the part in hair (see photos). Sew cast-on edges to top and sides of head. If hair fronts stick up too much, add a few more sts between bottom surfaces of hair fronts and upper forehead.

Face details

With B, embroider mouth and laugh lines with long sts (see photos). Keep long st of mouth slightly loose for curved smile and apply a short st to center of mouth to maintain curve of yarn.

With B, short st under mouth for lower lip line. Short st under each eye for lower lid lines. With A, short sts between lower lid lines and bottoms of eyes. Straight stitch under mouth line.

With B, long st over each safety eye from lower outside corner to upper inside corner, allowing yarn to curve over top of eye. Hold yarn in place with a few short sts. With A, long st directly above long st in B, applying short sts over long st to hold shaping.

BODY

Legs

With C, cast on 14 sts and divide over 4 sts. Join, taking care not to twist sts, and pm for beg of rnd.

Inc rnd 1 [(Kfb) twice, k3, (kfb) twice] twice—22 sts.

Rnds 2 and 3 Knit.

Inc rnd 4 [(K2, M1R) twice, k3, (M1L, k2) twice] twice—30 sts.

Rnds 5–9 Knit.

Dec rnd 10 [K2tog] twice, k22, [ssk] twice—26 sts.

Cut yarn leaving a 12"/30.5cm tail.

Divide sts evenly over 2 needles, hold parallel, and join with Kitchener st until 8 sts rem on each needle—16 sts.

Join C to first st on front needle, leaving a long yarn tail, and cont as foll:

Rnds 11–20 Knit.

Cut C. Join A.

Rnds 21–40 Knit.

Cut A. Join E.

Rnds 41–45 Knit.

Rnd 46 K4, pm, k8, pm k4.

Cut E.

Redistribute sts evenly over 2 dpn with rnd 46 markers marking two 8-st groups. Front of foot is centered below one 8-st group. Set aside.

Work 2nd leg in same way.

Redistribute sts over 2 dpn in same manner as first leg with foot facing forward. Shift sts to left on needles and place first leg onto needles so both feet face forward. Two legs are now on your needles—32 sts.

Torso

With E, work in the rnd as foll:

Rnd 47 Knit across front edge of first leg, front edge of 2nd leg, back edge of 2nd leg, and back edge of first leg—32 sts.

Inc rnd 48 [K2, M1R, k4, M1R, k4, M1L, k4, M1L, k2] twice —40 sts.

Rnds 49–54 Knit.

Dec rnd 55 [K2, k2tog, k12, ssk, k2] twice—38 sts.

Rnds 56–58 Knit.

Dec rnd 59 K20, k2tog, k2, k2tog, k4, ssk, k2, ssk, k2—34 sts.

Rnds 60–64 Knit.

Rnd 65 K2, k2tog, k10, ssk, k4, k2tog, k8, ssk, k2—30 sts.

Rnds 66–74 Knit.

Shoulder Openings

Dec row 75 K2, k2tog, k8, ssk, k2, turn, leaving rem 14 back sts unworked.

Cont over front sts only as foll:

Row 76 Purl.

Rows 77–82 Work even in St st (k on RS, p on WS).
Cut yarn and place sts on holder.

Join E to back sts and work over 14 unworked back sts only as foll:
Dec row 75 K2, k2tog, k6, ssk, k2—12 sts.
Row 76 Purl.
Rows 77–82 Work even in St st.
Cut yarn.

Shoulders
Join E and cont to work in rnds over all 26 sts as foll:
Rnd 83 Knit.
Dec rnd 84 [K1, k2tog] twice, k2, ssk, k1, ssk, k2, k2tog, k6, ssk, k1—20 sts.
Rnd 85 Knit.
Dec rnd 86 [(K2tog) twice, k2, (ssk) twice] twice—12 sts.
Cut E. Join A.
Rnds 87–91 Knit.
Bind off.

Arms and Hands
**With E, cast on 14 sts and divide over 3 dpn. Join, taking care not to twist sts, and pm for beg of rnd.
Rnds 1–30 Knit.
Dec rnd 31 [K1, k2tog, k1, ssk, k1] twice—10 sts.
Cut E. Join A.
Rnds 32–35 Knit.
Inc rnd 36 [K1, M1R, k3, M1L, k1] twice—14 sts.
Rnd 37 Knit.

Thumb opening
Rnd 38 Yo, k2tog, k to end.
Rnd 39 K into yo space, k13.

Hand
Rnds 40–42 Knit.
Dec rnd 43 [K3, SKP, k2] twice—12 sts.
Rnd 44 Knit.
Dec rnd 45 [K2tog, k2, ssk] twice—8 sts.
Cut yarn leaving a 12"/30.5cm tail.
With sts divided evenly over 2 needles, hold parallel and join using Kitchener st.

Thumb
Rnd 1 With A and 3 dpn, pick up and k 6 sts around thumb opening space on side of hand.
Rnds 2–4 Knit.
Cut yarn and thread tail through rem 6 sts. Pull tightly to close.
Rep from ** beg for 2nd arm and hand.

Body assembly
Note If inserting wire, it may be helpful to use a long, thin tool, such as a chopstick, to help work stuffing in around wire. Do not close up feet or arms entirely until you are satisfied with how each limb is stuffed.

If not inserting wire, simply stuff pieces and sew in place, making sure feet face forward and thumbs point upward.

If wiring toy, shape end of wire into a 1"/2.5cm oval-shaped loop on one end and insert into leg through bottom of foot, allowing 2–3"/5–7.5cm of wire to exit through top of neck. Rep with 2nd wire through opposite foot. Bend oval-shaped loops to sit flat on floor (like feet) and insert stuffing into feet and legs. Sew bottoms of feet closed. Stuff body.
With 3rd wire, make a small loop at one end to palce inside hand. Insert into one arm and add stuffing around wire, allowing end of wire to stick out. Sew edge of arm opening to arm opening on body, taking care to orient arm with thumb pointed up. The wire should pass through body and stick out other arm hole.
Shape end of exposed wire into a loop for other hand, trimming excess length, if necessary. Slide 2nd arm over wire and add stuffing. Sew edge of arm opening to arm opening on body.

For wired or unwired toy, close any other openings or holes on body. Weave in yarn ends, leaving neck open.

PANTS
Legs
With D, cast on 20 sts and divide evenly over 2 dpn. Join, taking care not to twist sts, and pm for beg of rnd.
Rnds 1–36 Knit.
Cut yarn leaving a 12"/30.5cm tail and place sts on 2 st holders.
Make a 2nd pant leg and cut yarn.
Shift 2nd pant leg sts to left on needles and transfer first pant leg sts onto needles—40 sts in total with 20 sts on each needle.

Pant
Rnd 37 With D, knit across front edge of first pant leg, knit across front edge of 2nd pant leg, knit across back edge of 2nd pant leg, and knit across back edge of first pant leg—40 sts.
Inc rnd 38 [K2, M1R, k4, M1R, k8, M1L, k4, M1L, k2] twice —48 sts.
Rnds 39–44 Knit.
Dec rnd 45 [K2, k2tog, k16, ssk, k2] twice—44 sts.
Rnd 46 Knit.
Rnd 47 [K2, k2tog, k14, ssk, k2] twice—40 sts.
Bind off very loosely. Cut yarn and weave in ends.

TIE

With F, cast on 8 sts and divide evenly over 2 dpn. Join, taking care not to twist sts, and pm for beg of rnd.

Rnd 1 Knit.

Inc rnd 2 [K1, M1R, k2, M1L, k1] twice—12 sts.

Rnds 3 and 4 Knit.

Dec rnd 5 [K1, k2tog, ssk, k1] twice—8 sts.

Rnds 6–15 Knit.

Inc rnd 16 [K1, M1R, k2, M1L, k1] twice—12 sts.

Rnds 17–30 Knit.

Dec rnd 31 [K1, k2tog, ssk, k1] twice—8 sts.

Rnd 32 Knit.

Rnd 33 [K2tog, ssk] twice—4 sts.

Cut yarn and thread tail through rem 4 sts. Pull tightly to close.

Tightly wind strand of F around rnd 5 of tie to cinch tie knot shaping. Tie off and sew in ends.

Attach top of tie knot to front of body at last rnd of E at base of neck.

SHIRT COLLAR

With E, cast on 18 sts.

Row 1 Knit.

Row 2 Purl.

Inc row 3 K1, M1R, k16, M1L, k1—20 sts.

Rows 4–6 Work even in St st.

Inc row 7 K1, M1R, k18, M1L, k1—22 sts.

Rows 8–10 Work even in St st.

Bind off.

Place knit side of collar against back of neck. Sew cast-on edge to last E rnd of body at base of neck on either side of tie knot. Fold collar down and tack in place.

CARDIGAN

Note When indicated in pattern, place removable markers on sts and leave in place until assembling cardigan.

Back

With G, cast on 27 sts.

Row 1 (WS) *K1, p1; rep from * to last st, k1.

Row 2 *P1, k1; rep from * to last st, p1.

Row 3 Rep row 1.

Rows 4–27 Work even in St st.

Dec row 28 K1, pm, k2tog, k21, ssk, k1, pm—25 sts.

Row 29 Purl.

Dec row 30 K1, k2tog, k19, ssk, k1—23 sts.

Row 31 Purl.

Dec row 32 K1, k2tog, k17, ssk, k1—21 sts.

Row 33 Purl.

Dec row 34 K1, k2tog, k15, ssk, k1—19 sts.

Rows 35–37 Work even in St st.

Row 38 K6, turn, leaving rem sts on hold.

Rows 39–41 Work even in St st over 6 sts, bind off. Rejoin yarn to rem sts on back.

Row 38 (cont) Bind off next 7 sts and fasten off yarn—6 sts rem on LH needle. Cut yarn.
Rejoin yarn to rem sts on back.

Row 38 (cont) Knit.

Rows 39–41 Work even in St st over rem 6 sts. Bind off, leaving a long tail for seaming

Right front

With G, cast on 13 sts.

Row 1 (WS) *K1, p1; rep from * to last st, k1.

Row 2 *P1, k1; rep from * to last st, p1.

Row 3 Rep row 1.

Rows 4–27 Work even in St st.

Dec row 28 K10, ssk, k1, pm—12 sts.

Row 29 and all rem WS rows Purl.

Dec row 30 K9, ssk, k1—11 sts.

Dec row 32 K8, ssk, k1—10 sts.

Dec row 34 K7, ssk, k1—9 sts.

Dec row 36 K1, pm, k2tog, k6—8 sts.

Dec row 38 K1, k2tog, k5—7 sts.

Dec row 40 K1, k2tog, k4—6 sts.

Row 41 Purl.

Bind off, leaving a long tail for seaming.

Left Front

With G, cast on 13 sts.

Rows 1–27 Work same as for right front.

Dec row 28 (RS) K1, pm, k2tog, k10—12 sts.

Row 29 and all rem WS rows Purl.

Dec row 30 K1, k2tog, k9—11 sts.

Dec row 32 K1, k2tog, k8—10 sts.

Dec row 34 K1, k2tog, k7—9 sts.

Dec row 36 K6, ssk, k1, pm—8 sts.

Dec row 38 K5, ssk, k1—7 sts.

Dec row 40 K4, ssk, k1—6 sts.

Row 41 Purl.

Bind off, leaving a long tail for seaming.

Sleeves

With G, cast on 26 sts.

Rows 1–3 *K1, p1; rep from * to end.

Rows 4–23 Beg with a knit row, work even in St st.

Inc row 24 (RS) K1, M1R, k24, M1L, k1—28 sts.
Rows 25–29 Work even in St st.
Inc row 30 K1, M1R, k26, M1L, k1—30 sts.
Row 31 Purl.
Bind off, leaving a long tail for seaming

Cardigan assembly
Sew shoulder seams. Center bound-off edges of sleeves between markers on fronts and back. Sew sleeves in place and remove markers. Sew side and underarm seams.

Trim and collar
With G, RS facing, and beg at lower edge of right front, pick up and k 16 sts along right front, 29 sts along upper right front, back, and upper left front, and 16 sts along left front—61 sts.
Row 1 (WS) [K1, p1] 22 times, k1, w&t, [p1, k1] 13 times, p1, w&t, [k1, p1] 22 times, k1.
Bind off in rib. Weave in ends.
Place cardigan on doll and sew front edges tog from bottom to about halfway up (tucking tie inside cardigan).

Zipper
With I, embroider chain sts from bottom of cardigan to where fronts are no longer seamed, then embroider zipper details from split to short-row shaping of collar.
For zipper pull, fold an 8"/20.5cm length of I in half and knot ¼"/1cm above fold point. Attach knot at top of line of chain sts.

SNEAKERS
With E, cast on 20 sts and divide evenly over 4 dpn. Join, taking care not to twist sts, and pm for beg of rnd (front of shoe).
Inc rnd 1 [(Kfb) twice, k6, (kfb) twice] twice—28 sts.
Rnd 2 Knit.
Inc rnd 3 [Kfb] 4 times, k8, [kfb] 4 times, k8, [kfb] 4 times —40 sts.
Rnd 4 Knit.
Rnds 5 and 6 Purl.
Cut E. Join F.
Rnd 7 Knit.
Dec rnd 8 [K2tog] 3 times, k28, [ssk] 3 times—34 sts.
Rnds 9 and 10 Knit.
Dec rnd 11 [K2tog] twice, k26, [ssk] twice—30 sts.
Rnds 12 and 13 Knit.
Dec rnd 14 [K2tog] twice, k22, [ssk] twice—26 sts.
Rnd 15 Knit.
Rnd 16 [K2tog] twice, k18, [ssk] twice—22 sts.
Bind off loosely. Weave in ends.

With E, sew cast-on edge tog from front to back of shoe.
Cut a length of E and embroider on lace details, tying ends into a bow at top of shoe. Tie a knot at each end of lace to keep yarn from fraying.
Rep for 2nd shoe.

LOAFERS
With B, cast on 20 sts and divide evenly over 4 dpn. Join, taking care not to twist sts, and pm for beg of rnd (front of shoe).
Inc rnd 1 [(Kfb) twice, k6, (kfb) twice] twice—28 sts.
Rnd 2 Knit.
Inc rnd 3 [(Kfb) 4 times, k8] twice, [kfb] 4 times—40 sts.
Rnd 4 Knit.
Rnd 5 Purl.
Cut B. Join H.
Rnd 6 Knit
Dec rnd 7 [K2tog] 3 times, k28, [ssk] 3 times—34 sts.
Rnds 8 and 9 Knit.
Dec rnd 10 [K2tog] twice, k26, [ssk] twice—30 sts.
Rnd 11 P8, k14, p8.
Rnds 12 and 13 Knit.
Dec rnd 14 [K2tog] twice, k22, [ssk] twice—26 sts.
Rnd 15 Knit.
Rnd 16 K6, bind off next 14 sts, k to end—12 sts.
Cut yarn, leaving a long tail.
Place rem 6 sts at beg of rnd on a dpn and last 6 sts of rnd on 2nd dpn. Hold needles tog and use long tail to graft sts tog with Kitchener st. Weave in ends.

Strap
With H, cast on 10 sts.
Purl 1 row. Bind off knitwise.
Place strap across top of loafer and secure in place. Weave in ends.

DANIEL STRIPED TIGER PUPPET

With J, cast on 20 sts and divide evenly over 4 dpn. Join, taking care not to twist sts, and pm for beg of rnd.

Rnds 1–10 Knit.

Inc rnd 11 [Kfb, M1R, k8, M1L, kfb] twice—28 sts.

Inc rnd 12 [Kfb, k12, kfb] twice—32 sts.

Rnd 13 Knit.

Dec rnd 14 [(K2tog) twice, k8, (ssk) twice] twice—24 sts.

Dec rnd 15 [(K2tog) twice, k4, (ssk) twice] twice—16 sts.

Dec rnd 16 [K2tog, k4, ssk] twice—12 sts.

Inc rnd 17 [K1, M1R, k4, M1L, k1] twice—16 sts.

Note Work foll short-row section carefully to shape nose. See page 127 for instructions on how to work wrap & turn (w&t).

Short-row 18 (RS) K6, w&t.

Short-row 19 P6, w&t.

Short-row 20 K5, w&t.

Short-row 21 P4, w&t.

Short-row 22 K3, w&t.

Short-row 23 P2, w&t.

Rnd 24 K to end of rnd, picking up wraps as you come to them. This completes nose shaping.

Rnd 25 Knit, picking up rem wraps as you come to them.

Rnds 26 and 27 Knit.

Dec rnd 28 [K2tog, k4, ssk] twice—12 sts.

Rnd 29 Knit.

Cut yarn, thread tail through rem sts, and pull to close.

Ears

With J, cast on 4 sts and divide evenly over 2 dpn. Join, taking care not to twist sts, and pm for beg of rnd.

Inc rnd 1 [Kfb] 4 times—8 sts.

Rnd 2 Knit.

Hold needles tog and bind off using 3-needle bind-off.

Sew cast-on edge tog.

Rep for 2nd ear.

Puppet assembly

Note See photos for reference.

Sew bound-off edge of ears to sides of head. Weave in ends.

Add 4mm safety eyes above nose shaping, 1 or 2 sts apart. Stuff head lightly and apply a few sts between front and back of neck to hold stuffing in place.

With pink embroidery thread, embroider a small, triangle-shaped nose on front of nose shaping. With black embroidery thread, embroider mouth and bottom edges nose.

For whiskers, tie three 6"/15cm lengths of white thread to back of neck and draw threads through sides of nose. Trim each tread to ½"/1.5cm.

With white embroidery thread, apply a French knot to back of left wrist. With black embroidery floss, embroider straight stitches around wrist for watch band and 3 straight sts over ends of each arm for paw details. With gold embroidery thread, embroider short sts around French knot to outline watch face. ■

"*You rarely have time for everything you want in this life, so you need to make choices. And hopefully your choices can come from a deep sense of who you are.*"

Living Room Stoplight

DESIGNED BY Megan Kreiner

This adorable stoplight begins with the column, worked in the round while slipping the contrasting cement color to create the vertical mortar details. The stoplight base and traffic lights are worked in the round, using short rows to create the hood details.

■◖■■▷

FINISHED MEASUREMENTS

Height 6"/15cm
Width 2½"/6.5cm
Depth 4¼"/10.5cm

Materials

• 1 3½oz/100g hank (approx 220yd/200m) of Cascade Yarns *Cascade 220* (Peruvian highland wool) each in #2413 Red (A), #9499 Sand (B), #9463B Gold (C), #7812 Lagoon (D), #9669 Gold Fusion (E), and #8895 Christmas Red (F) **④**
• One set (4) size 4 (3.5mm) double pointed needles, *or size to obtain gauge*
• Stitch markers
• Stitch holders
• Foam stabilizer
• 1"/2.5cm thick cushion foam
• Small amount of polyester stuffing
• Tapestry Needle

GAUGE

24 sts and 34 rnds to 4"/10cm over St st using size 4 (3.5 mm) needles.
Gauge is not vital for this project, but it is best to keep stitches tight to keep stuffing from showing through.

STOPLIGHT
BRICK COLUMN

With A, cast on 8 sts and divide evenly over 4 dpn. Join, taking care not to twist sts, and pm for beg of rnd.
Inc rnd 1 Kfb in each st around—16 sts.
Rnds 2, 4, 6, and 8 Knit.

Inc rnd 3 [Kfb, M1, k3] 4 times —24 sts.
Inc rnd 5 [K1, kfb, M1, k4] 4 times —32 sts.
Inc rnd 7 [K2, kfb, M1, k5] 4 times —40 sts.
Inc rnd 9 [K3, kfb, M1, k6] 4 times —48 sts.
Rnd 10 Purl.
Join B.
Rnds 11 and 12 With B, knit.
Rnd 13 With A, [k3, sl 1 wyib, k2] 8 times.
Rnds 14–17 With A, [p3, sl 1 wyib, p2] 8 times.
Rnds 18 and 19 With B, knit.
Rnd 20 With A, [sl 1 wyib, k5] 8 times.
Rnds 21–24 With A, [sl 1 wyib, p5] 8 times.
Rnds 25–80 Rep rnds 11–24 four times more.
Rnds 81 and 82 With B, knit.
Cut B.
Cut ten 2¼"/5.5cm squares of cushion foam. Stack and insert into brick.
Cont with A only as foll:
Rnd 83 Knit.
Rnd 84 Purl.
Dec rnd 85 [K3, k3tog, k6] 4 times—40 sts.
Rnd 86 Knit.
Dec rnd 87 [K2, k3tog, k5] 4 times—32 sts.
Rnd 88 Knit.
Dec rnd 89 [K1, k3tog, k4] 4 times—24 sts.
Rnd 90 Knit.
Dec rnd 91 [K3tog, k3] 4 times—16 sts.
Rnd 92 Knit.
Cut yarn and weave through rem 16 sts. Pull tightly to close hole.

*During the opening sequence of Mister Rogers'
Neighborhood, the stoplight in the living room
was always yellow. It was a reminder to viewers
to slow down, perhaps even just a little.*

STOPLIGHT BASE

With C, cast on 30 sts and divide evenly over 3 dpn. Join, taking care not to twist sts, and pm for beg of rnd.

Rnds 1–15 [K1, p1, k12, p1] twice.

Rnd 16 [K1, p14] twice.

Rep rnds 1–16 twice more.

Bind off and cut yarn, leaving a long tail for sewing.

Cut two 1½ x 5½"/4 x 14cm rectangles of foam stabilizer. Stack and insert into base.

Sew halves of cast-on edge tog to close off. Rep for bound-off edge. Attach to narrower side of brick column.

LIGHTS

(make 1 each in D, E, and F)

With D, E, or F, cast on 5 sts and divide over 3 dpn. Join, taking care not to twist sts, and pm for beg of rnd.

Inc rnd 1 Kfb in each st around—10 sts.

Rnd 2 Knit.

Inc rnd 3 [K1, M1] 10 times—20 sts.

Rnds 4–6 Knit.

Cut D, E, or F.

Light Hood

Join C.

Rnd 7 Knit.

Short-row 8 (RS) K8, w&t (see page 127).

Short-row 9 (WS) P6, w&t.

Short-row 10 K5, w&t.

Short-row 11 P4, w&t.

Short-row 12 K7, picking up wraps as you knit, turn.

Short-row 13 P10, picking up wraps as you purl, turn.

Short-row 14 K10, turn.

Short-row 15 P10, turn.

Short-rows 16–19 Rep short-rows 14 and 15 twice more.

Bind off 10 sts purlwise, pick up and bind off 3 sts along side edge of 10-st flap, bind off rem 10 sts purlwise, pick up and bind off 3 sts along other side edge of 10-st flap.

Fold hood flap back and sew bound-off edge of hood to rnd 7.

With C, sew red light in center of top square of light base, inserting a bit of stuffing as you go. Rep for yellow light in center square and green light in bottom square of light base. ∎

"How many times have you noticed that it's the little quiet moments in the midst of life that seem to give the rest extra-special meaning?"

Mini-Cardigans

DESIGNED BY Linda M. Perry

These mini-cardigans make for quick projects. Knit some for dolls, decorations for a Christmas tree, motifs for a baby mobile, or even to string together as a garland. Mini-hangers can be purchased or shaped out of crafting wire for extra fun.

FINISHED MEASUREMENTS

Width (cuff to cuff) 6¼"/16cm
Length 3¾"/9.5cm

MATERIALS

• 1 1¾oz/50g hank (approx 166yd/152m) of Jagger Spun *Maine Line ⅜ Sport* (wool) each in Iris (A), Marigold (B), Garnet (C), and Emerald (C) 2
• One pair of size 3 (3.25mm) needles, *or size to obtain gauge*
• One set (4) of size 3 (3.25mm) double-pointed needles (dpn)
• Stitch markers
• Two small stitch holders

GAUGE

24 sts and 32 rows to 4"/10cm over St st using size 3 (3.25mm) needles.
Take time to check gauge.

NOTE

1) Cardigan is worked from the top down, using straight needles for the body and double-pointed needles for the sleeves.
2) One hank of yarn will make multiple cardigans. Make as many as you wish and are able from each color.
3) If desired, use embroidery thread to add zipper details to fronts.

Cardigan
YOKE

With straight needles, cast on 15 sts.
Rows 1 and 2 Knit.
Row 3 (RS) K3, pm, k2, pm, k5, pm, k2, pm, k3.
Row 4 Purl.
Inc row 5 [K to 1 st before marker, kfb, sm, kfb] 4 times, k to end—8 sts inc'd.
Rep last 2 rows 4 times more—55 sts in total with 8 sts per front, 12 sts per sleeve, and 15 sts for back

LEFT FRONT

Row 1 (RS) K12, turn, leaving rem sts on hold.
Work even in St st (k on RS, p on WS) for 11 rows more.
Knit 3 rows for lower edge.
Bind off.
With RS facing, place next 12 sts for sleeve on holder.

BACK

With RS facing, join yarn to rem sts.
Row 1 (RS) K15, turn, leaving rem sts on hold.
Work even in St st for 11 rows more.
Knit 3 rows for lower edge. Bind off.

With RS facing, place next 12 sts for sleeve on holder.

RIGHT FRONT

With RS facing, join yarn to rem sts.
Row 1 (RS) Knit.
Work even in St st for 11 rows more.
Knit 3 rows for lower edge. Bind off.

SLEEVES

Divide 12 sts for one sleeve evenly over 3 dpn. Join and pm to mark beg of rnd.
Rnds 1 and 2 Knit.
Dec rnd 3 K to last 2 sts, k2tog—1 st dec'd.
Rnds 4–8 Rep dec rnd 3 five times more—6 sts.
Rnd 9 Purl.
Rnd 10 Knit.
Rnd 11 Purl.
Bind off knitwise.
Rep for rem sleeve.

FINISHING

Weave in ends. Steam lightly. Sew side seams. ∎

"In times of stress, the best thing we can do for each other is to listen with our ears and our hearts and to be assured that our questions are just as important as our answers."

NEIGHBORHOOD TROLLEY

Blankets

Warm hearts and homes with a duo of quick and chunky throws that memorialize the words of Mister Rogers. Don't forget about baby with a mural-like blanket that is sure to become a cherished heirloom.

Won't You Be My Neighbor Blanket

DESIGNED BY Katherine Mehls

Mister Rogers' words stand out—literally—in this blanket. Worked in one piece in a bulky yarn, each word appears in three-dimensional garter ridges on a field of Stockinette stitch. Garter borders add an endearing complement.

FINISHED MEASUREMENTS
48"/122cm square

MATERIALS
• 11 3½oz/100g balls (each approx 106yd/96m) of Universal Yarn *Deluxe Bulky Superwash* (superwash wool) in #915 Teal Vipers (5)
• One size 11 (4.5mm) circular needle, 32"/80cm long, *or size to obtain gauge*

GAUGE
12 sts and 18 rows to 4"/10cm over St st using size 11 (8mm) needle.
Take time to check gauge.

NOTES
1) Circular needle is used to accommodate the large number of stitches. Do not join.
2) The words that appear in each chart are created on the wrong side. Simply knit every right side row throughout the entire blanket.

BLANKET
Cast on 143 sts. Knit 10 rows.

DIVIDER SECTION
Row 1 (RS) Knit.
Row 2 K5 (garter st border), p to last 5 sts, k5 (garter st border).
Rows 3–12 Rep rows 1 and 2 five times more.

CHART 1
Row 1 (RS) Knit.
Row 2 K5, p5, work row 2 of chart 1 over 123 sts, p to last 5 sts, k5.
Cont in pats as established, keeping first and last 5 sts in garter st (k every row) and rem sts outside of chart in St st (k on RS, p on WS) through row 28 of chart 1.

Rep rows 1–12 of divider section.

CHART 2
Row 1 (RS) Knit.
Row 2 K5, p5, work row 2 of chart 2 over 27 sts, p to last 5 sts, k5. Cont in pats as established through row 28 of chart 2.

Rep rows 1–12 of divider section.

CHART 3
Row 1 (RS) Knit.
Row 2 K5, p5, work row 2 of chart 3 over 27 sts, p to last 5 sts, k5. Cont in pats as established through row 28 of chart 3.

Rep rows 1–12 of divider section.

CHART 4
Row 1 (RS) Knit.
Row 2 K5, p5, work row 2 of chart 4 over 42 sts, p to last 5 sts, k5. Cont in pats as established through row 28 of chart 4.

Rep rows 1–12 of divider section.

CHART 5
Row 1 (RS) Knit.
Row 2 K5, p5, work row 2 of chart 5 over 65 sts, p to last 5 sts, k5. Cont in pats as established through row 28 of chart 5.

Rep rows 1–12 of divider section.

Knit 9 rows. Bind off loosely knitwise on WS.

FINISHING
Weave in ends. Block to measurements. ∎

CHART 2

STITCH KEY

☐ k on RS, p on WS

⊟ k on WS

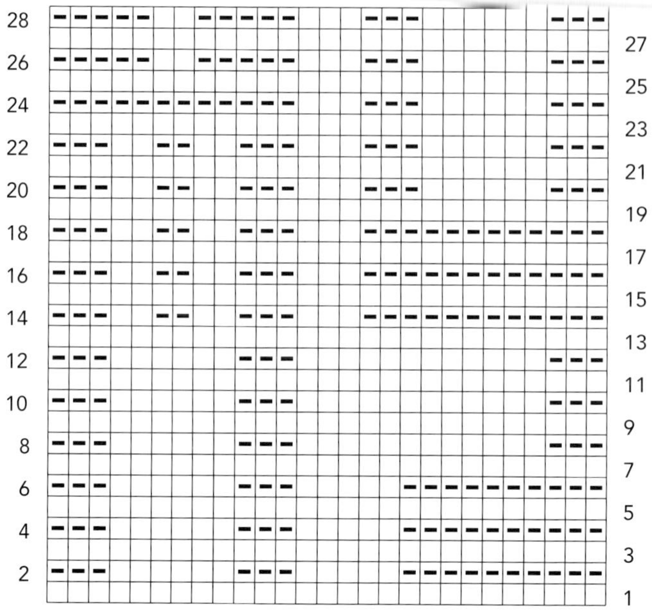

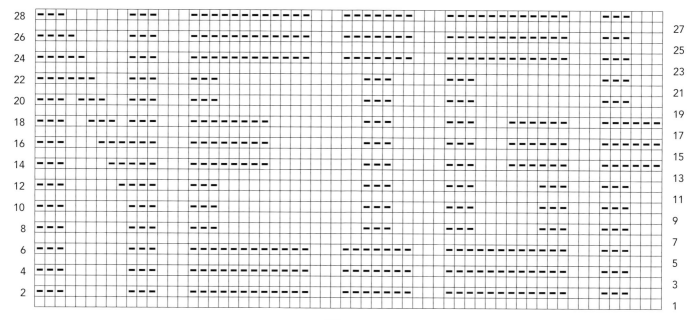

27 sts

CHART 1 – LEFT HALF

123 sts

CHART 3

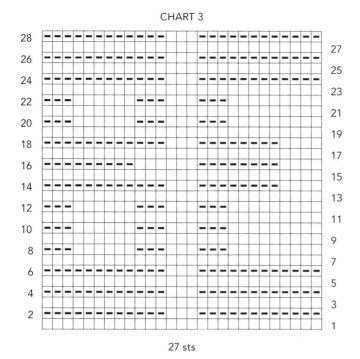

27 sts

> *"The world needs a sense of worth, and it will achieve it only by its people feeling that they are worthwhile."*

CHART 1 – RIGHT HALF

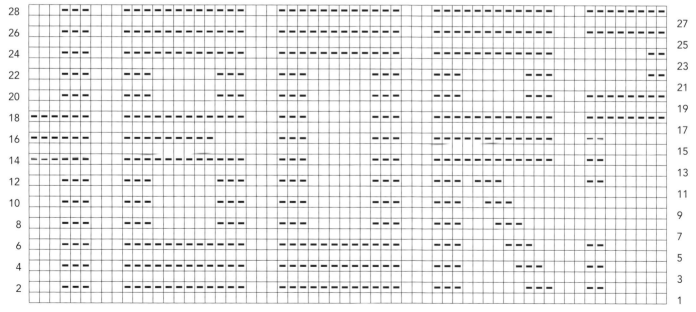

123 sts

CHART 5

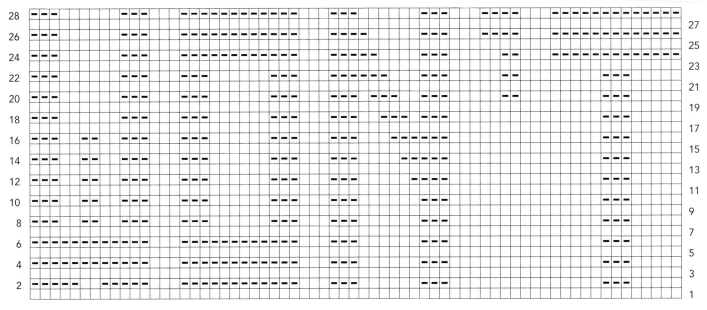

65 sts

STITCH KEY

☐ k on RS, p on WS

⊟ k on WS

CHART 4

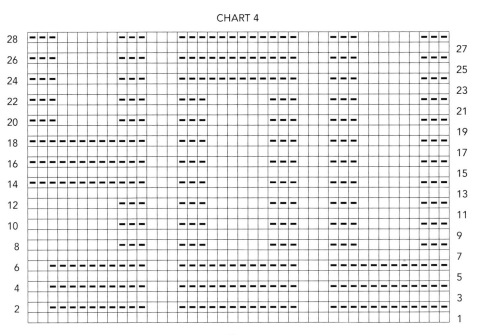

42 sts

Lyrics from the song "Won't You Be My Neighbor?"

I have always wanted to have a neighbor just like you!

I've always wanted to live in a neighborhood with you.

So let's make the most of this beautiful day.

Since we're together we might as well say,

Would you be mine?

Could you be mine?

Won't you be my neighbor?

I Like You Blanket

DESIGNED BY Katherine Mehls

This throw knits up quickly in a bulky-weight yarn, worked from bottom to top in a single piece. The border and lettering are worked in garter stitch for a graphic, dimensional, and simple aesthetic.

FINISHED MEASUREMENTS
48"/122cm square

MATERIALS
• 11 3½oz/100g balls (each approx 106yd/96m) of Universal Yarn *Deluxe Bulky Superwash* (superwash wool) in #926 Auburn ⬛
• One size 11 (4.5mm) circular needle, 32"/80cm long, *or size to obtain gauge*

GAUGE
12 sts and 18 rows to 4"/10cm over St st using size 11 (8mm) needle.
Take time to check gauge.

NOTES
1) Circular needle is used to accommodate the large number of stitches. Do not join.
2) The words that appear in each chart are created on the wrong side. Simply knit every right side row throughout the entire blanket.

BLANKET
Cast on 139 sts. Knit 10 rows.

DIVIDER SECTION
Row 1 (RS) Knit.
Row 2 K5 (garter st border), p to last 5 sts, k5 (garter st border).
Rows 3–12 Rep rows 1 and 2 five times more.

CHART 1
Row 1 (RS) Knit.
Row 2 K5, p18, work row 2 of chart 1 over 93 sts, p to last 5 sts, k5.
Cont in pats as established, keeping first and last 5 sts in garter st (k every row) and rem sts outside of chart in St st (k on RS, p on WS) through row 28 of chart 1.

Rep rows 1–12 of divider section.

CHART 2
Row 1 (RS) Knit.
Row 2 K5, p17, work row 2 of chart 2 over 94 sts, p to last 5 sts, k5.
Cont in pats as established through row 28 of chart 2.

Rep rows 1–12 of divider section.

CHART 3
Row 1 (RS) Knit.
Row 2 (WS) K5, p18, work row 2 of chart 3 over 58 sts, p to last 5 sts, k5.
Cont in pats as established through row 28 of chart 3.

Rep rows 1–12 of divider section.

CHART 4
Row 1 (RS) Knit.
Row 2 K5, p18, work row 2 of chart 4 over 42 sts, p to last 5 sts, k5.
Cont in pats as established through row 28 of chart 4.

Rep rows 1–12 of divider section.

CHART 5
Row 1 (RS) Knit.
Row 2 K5, p18, work row 2 of chart 5 over 68 sts, p to last 5 sts, k5.
Cont in pats as established through row 28 of chart 5.

Rep rows 1–12 of divider section.

Knit 9 rows. Bind off loosely knitwise on WS.

FINISHING
Weave in ends. Block to measurements. ■

Mister Rogers adored his grandfather, who once told him "Freddy, I like you just the way you are!" That phrase had quite an impact on the young Mister Rogers and became a loving motto that he shared with viewers many times.

STITCH KEY

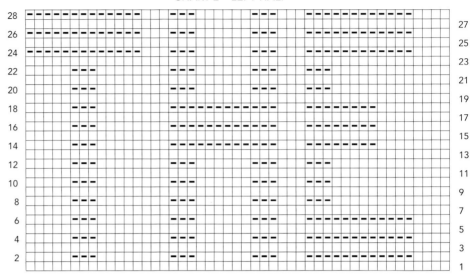

☐	k on RS, p on WS
⊟	k on WS

CHART 2 – LEFT HALF

94 sts

CHART 1 – LEFT HALF

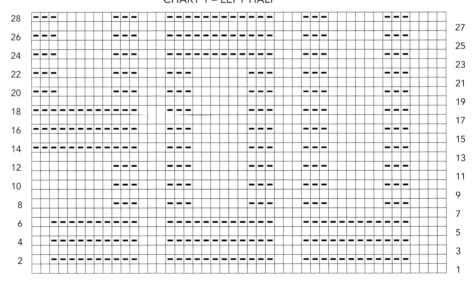

93 sts

CHART 2 – RIGHT HALF

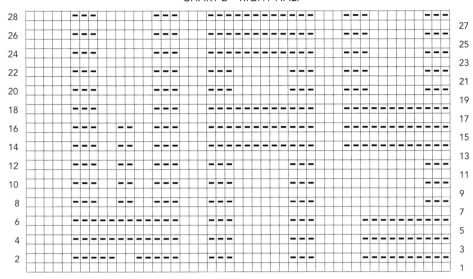

94 sts

CHART 1 – RIGHT HALF

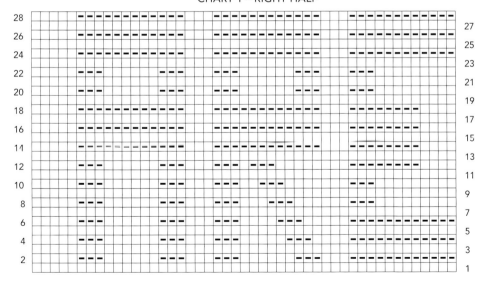

93 sts

CHART 4

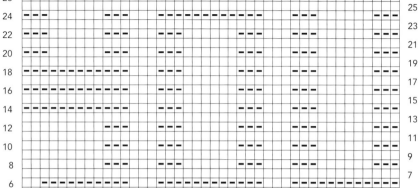

42 sts

CHART 3

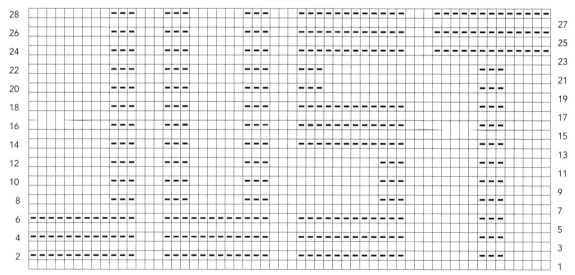

58 sts

STITCH KEY

☐ k on RS, p on WS

▬ k on WS

CHART 5

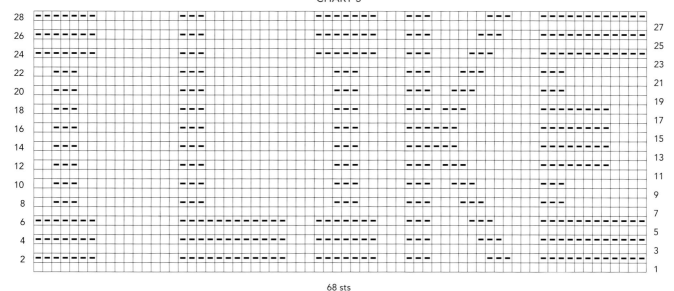

68 sts

I don't think anyone can grow unless he's loved exactly as he is now, appreciated for what he is rather than what he will be.

Neighborhood Trolley Baby Blanket

DESIGNED BY Amy Bahrt

Three vignettes of the cheery Neighborhood Trolley traveling from Mister Rogers' neighborhood to the Neighborhood of Make-Believe are stacked on a single baby blanket for triple the delight.

FINISHED MEASUREMENTS

25 x 30"/63.5 x 76cm

MATERIALS

- 3 3½oz/100g balls (each approx 220yd/200m) of Cascade Yarns *220 Superwash* (superwash wool) each in #809 Really Red (A) and #280 Placid Blue (E)
- 1 ball each in #875 Feather Grey (B), #815 Black (C), #864 Christmas Green (D), #883 Puget Sound (F), #871 White (G), #1961 Camel (H), and #820 Lemon (I)
- One size 7 (4.5mm) circular needle, 32"/80cm long, *or size to obtain gauge*
- Black embroidery thread
- Embroidery needle
- One ³⁄₈"/10mm red button

GAUGE

20 sts and 26 rows to 4"/10cm over St st using size 7 (4.5mm) needle.
Take time to check gauge.

NOTES

1) For border, work first and last 5 stitches of every row in garter st (k every row) with A.
2) Charts are worked in Stockinette stitch using separate balls of yarn for each block of color. When changing colors, twist yarns on wrong side to prevent holes in work.
3) "NEIGHBORHOOD TROLLEY" is embroidered onto blanket during finishing.
4) Circular needle is used to accommodate the large number of stitches. Do not join.

BLANKET

With circular needle and A, cast on 125 sts.
Knit 10 rows for lower garter st border.

PANEL 1

Rows 1–4 With A, k5 (garter border); with B, work in St st (k on RS, p on WS) to last 5 sts; with A, k5 (garter border).

Rows 5 and 6 Rep row 1, using C instead of B.
Row 7 (RS) With A, k5; with B, k9, pm; work row 1 of chart 1 over 46 sts, pm; with B, k to last 5 sts; with A, k5.
Row 8 With A, k5; with B, p to marker, sm; work next row of chart 1, sm; with B, p to last 5 sts; with A, k5.
Rows 9 and 10 Cont as established with background color in C.
Rows 11–14 Cont as established with background color in B.
Rows 15–20 Cont as established with background color in D.
Row 21 (RS) With A, k5; with E, k9, sm, work next row of chart 1, sm; with E, k10, pm, work row 1 of chart 2 over 41 sts, pm; with E, k to last 5 sts; with A, k5.
Cont as established, working background color in E, through row 42 of chart 2, removing markers as you complete each chart.
Once both charts are complete, work 4 rows more with garter st borders in A and rem sts of blanket worked in St st with E.

PANEL 2

Rows 1–6 Work same as panel 1.
Row 7 (RS) With A, k5; with B, k35, pm; work row 1 of chart 1 over 46 sts, pm; with B, k to last 5 sts; with A, k5.
Row 8 With A, k5; with B, p to marker, sm; work next row of chart 1, sm; with B, p to last 5 sts; with A, k5.
Rows 9 and 10 Cont as established with background color in C.
Rows 11–14 Cont as established with background color in B.
Rows 15–20 Cont as established with background color in D.
Row 21 (RS) With A, k5; with E, k6, pm; work row 1 of chart 3 over 23 sts, pm; with E, k6, sm; work next row of chart 1, sm; with E, k6, pm; work row 1 of chart 3 over 23 sts, pm; with E, k to last 5 sts; with A, k5.

In one episode, Mister Rogers visited a trolley museum. He took Trolley with him and showed it to an expert who said it looked "just like a single-truck open-car like the St. Louis Car Company built around 1900."

Cont as established, working background color in E, through row 43 of chart 3, removing markers as you complete each chart.

Once all charts are complete, work 5 rows more with garter st borders in A and rem sts of blanket worked in St st with E.

PANEL 3

Rows 1–6 Work same as panel 1.

Row 7 (RS) With A, k5; with B, k60, pm; work row 1 of chart 1 over 46 sts, pm; with B, k to last 5 sts; with A, k5.

Row 8 With A, k5; with B, p to marker, sm; work next row of chart 1, sm; with B, p to last 5 sts; with A, k5.

Rows 9 and 10 Cont as established with background color in C.

Rows 11–14 Cont as established with background color in B.

Rows 15–20 Cont as established with background color in D.

Row 21 (RS) With A, k5; with E, k10, pm; work row 1 of chart 4 over 40 sts, pm; with E, k11, sm; with E, k10, sm; work next row of chart 1, sm; with E, k to last 5 sts; with A, k5.

COLOR & STITCH KEY

□	k on RS, p on WS

▨	A	▨	F
▨	B	□	G
■	C	▨	H
▨	D	▨	I
▨	E		

CHART 1

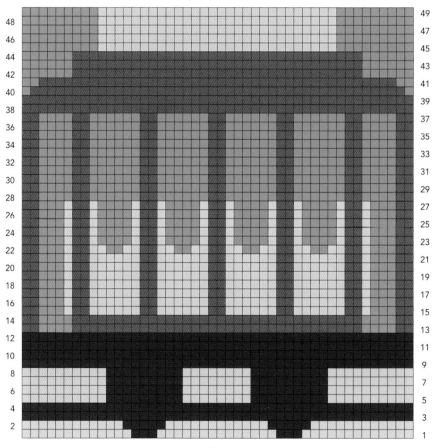

46 sts

Cont as established, working background color in E, through row 45 of chart 4, removing markers as you complete each chart.
Once both charts are complete, work 4 rows more with garter st borders in A and rem sts of blanket worked in St st with E.
With A only, knit 10 rows for top border.
Bind off.

FINISHING

Weave in ends. Block to measurements
With embroidery needle and 2 strands of embroidery thread held tog, embroider the words "NEIGHBORHOOD TROLLEY" on each of 3 yellow signs of chart 1 (see photos).
With 1 strand of B, embroider chain sts around bottom of each wheel for definition from "tracks" (see photos and page 126).
Sew button on door as indicated on Chart 4. ■

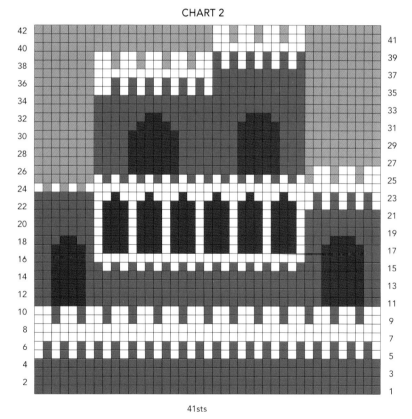

CHART 2

41sts

"The child is in me still . . . and sometimes not so still."

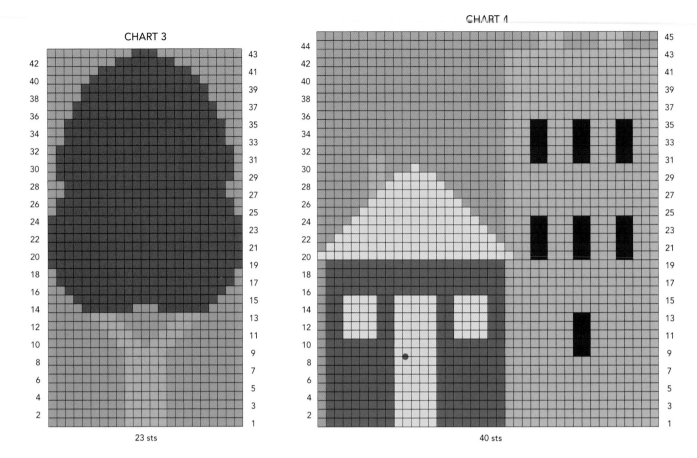

CHART 3

23 sts

CHART 4

40 sts

COLOR & STITCH KEY

☐ k on RS, p on WS

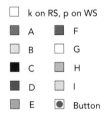

A	F
B	G
C	H
D	I
E	● Button

Helpful Information

ABBREVIATIONS

2nd	second
A, B	color A, B, etc.
beg	begin(ning)(s)
CC	contrast color
cont	continu(e)(es)(ing)
dec	decreas(e)(es)(ing)
dec'd	decreased
dpn	double-pointed needle(s)
foll	follow(ing)(s)
inc	increase(s)
inc'd	increased
k	knit
k2tog	knit 2 stitches together—1 stitch decreased
k3tog	knit 3 stitches together—2 stitches decreased
kfb	knit into front and back of same stitch—1 stitch increased
LH	left-hand
M1R	insert left needle from back to front under strand between last stitch worked and next stitch on left needle, knit into front loop to twist stitch—1 stitch increased
M1L	insert left needle from front to back under strand between last stitch worked and next stitch on LH needle, knit into back loop to twist stitch—1 stitch increased
M1P	insert left needle from front to back under strand between last st worked and next stitch on LH needle, purl strand through back loop—1 purl stitch increased
MC	main color
p	purl
p2tog	purl 2 stitches together—1 stitch decreased
p3tog	purl 3 stitches together—2 stitches decreased
pfb	purl into front and back of same stitch—1 stitch increased
pm	place marker
rem	remain(ing)(s)
rev	reverse
RH	right-hand
rnd(s)	round(s)
RS	right side(s)
S2KP	slip 2 stitches together as if to knit, knit 1, pass 2 slipped stitches over knit stitch—2 stitches decreased
SKP	slip 1 stitch, knit 1 stitch, pass slipped stitch over knit stitch—1 stitch decreased
SK2P	slip 1 stitch, knit 2 stitches together, pass slipped stitch over 2 stitches knit together—2 stitches decreased
sl	slip
sm	slip marker
ssk	slip next 2 stitches knitwise one at a time, return slipped stitches to left-hand needle, knit these 2 stitches together—1 stitch decreased
sssk	slip next 3 stitches knitwise one at a time, insert tip of LH needle into fronts of these stitches and knit them together—2 stitches decreased
st(s)	stitch(es)
St st	Stockinette stitch
tbl	through back loop(s)
tog	together
WS	wrong side(s)
wyib	with yarn in back
wyif	with yarn in front
yo(s)	yarnover(s)

SKILL LEVELS

■☐☐☐

BASIC
Projects using basic stitches. May include basic increases and decreases.

■■☐☐

EASY
Projects may include simple stitch patterns, colorwork, and/or shaping.

■■■☐

INTERMEDIATE
Projects may include involved stitch patterns, colorwork, and/or shaping.

■■■■

COMPLEX
Projects may include complex stitch patterns, colorwork, and/or shaping using a variety of techniques and stitches simultaneously.

Knitting Needle Sizes

US	Metric
0	2mm
1	2.25mm
2	2.75mm
3	3.25mm
4	3.5mm
5	3.75mm
6	4mm
7	4.5mm
8	5mm
9	5.5mm
10	6mm
10$\frac{1}{2}$	6.5mm
11	8mm
13	9mm
15	10mm
17	12.75mm
19	15mm
35	19mm

STANDARD YARN WEIGHT SYSTEM

Categories of yarn, gauge ranges, and recommended needle and hook sizes

Yarn Weight Symbol & Category	0 Lace	1 Super Fine	2 Fine	3 Light	4 Medium	5 Bulky	6 Super Bulky	7 Jumbo
Type of Yarns in Category	Fingering 10-count crochet thread	Sock, Fingering, Baby	Sport, Baby	DK, Light Worsted	Worsted, Afghan, Aran	Chunky, Craft, Rug	Super Bulky, Roving	Jumbo, Roving
Knit Gauge Range* in Stockinette Stitch to 4 inches	33–40** sts	27–32 sts	23–26 sts	21–24 sts	16–20 sts	12–15 sts	7–11 sts	6 sts and fewer
Recommended Needle in Metric Size Range	1.5–2.25 mm	2.25—3.25 mm	3.25—3.75 mm	3.75—4.5 mm	4.5—5.5 mm	5.5—8 mm	8—12.75 mm	12.75 mm and larger
Recommended Needle U.S. Size Range	000–1	1 to 3	3 to 5	5 to 7	7 to 9	9 to 11	11 to 17	17 and larger
Crochet Gauge* Ranges in Single Crochet to 4 inch	32–42 double crochets**	21–32 sts	16–20 sts	12–17 sts	11–14 sts	8–11 sts	6–9 sts	5 sts and fewer
Recommended Hook in Metric Size Range	Steel*** 1.6–1.4 mm	2.25—3.5 mm	3.5—4.5 mm	4.5—5.5 mm	5.5—6.5 mm	6.5—9 mm	9—16 mm	16 mm and larger
Recommended Hook U.S. Size Range	Steel*** 6, 7, 8 Regular hook B–1	B–1 to E–4	E–4 to 7	7 to I–9	I–9 to K–10 1/2	K–10 1/2 to M–13	M–13 to Q	Q and larger

* GUIDELINES ONLY: The above reflect the most commonly used gauges and needle or hook sizes for specific yarn categories.

** Lace weight yarns are usually knitted or crocheted on larger needles and hooks to create lacy, openwork patterns. Accordingly, a gauge range is difficult to determine. Always follow the gauge stated in your pattern.

*** Steel crochet hooks are sized differently from regular hooks—the higher the number, the smaller the hook, which is the reverse of regular hook sizing

This Standards & Guidelines booklet and downloadable symbol artwork are available at: **YarnStandards.com**

RESOURCES

Berroco
berroco.com

Cascade Yarns
cascadeyarns.com

Dill Buttons of America
us.dill-buttons.com

JaggerSpun
jaggeryarn.com

Jody Long
knittingfever.com

Lion Brand Yarn
lionbrand.com

Sandnes Garn
motherknitter.com
sandnes-garn.com

Patons
yarnspirations.com

Rowan
knitrowan.com

Universal Yarn
universalyarn.com

Finishing

SEAMING

There are different ways to seam, or join, your knitted pieces together. Here are some helpful and common methods.

Mattress Stitch on Stockinette Stitch

This invisible vertical seam is worked from the right side and is used to join two side edges row by row. It hides any uneven selvage stitches and creates an invisible seam, making it appear that the knitting is continuous.

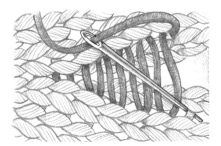

Insert the yarn needle under the horizontal bar between the first and second stitches. Insert the needle into the corresponding bar on the other piece. Continue alternating from side to side.

Mattress Stitch on Reverse Stockinette Stitch

As with stockinette stitch, this invisible seam is worked from the right side, row by row, but instead of working into the horizontal strand between stitches, work into the stitch itself. Alternate working into the top loop on one side with the bottom loop on the other side.

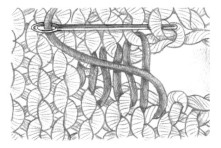

Working into the stitches inside the edge, insert the yarn needle into the top loop on one side, then in the bottom loop of the corresponding stitch on the other side. Continue to alternate in this way.

Invisible Horizontal Seam on Stockinette Stitch

This seam is used to join two bound-off edges, such as shoulder seams, and is worked stitch by stitch. You must have the same number of stitches on each piece. Pull the yarn tightly enough to hide the bound-off edges. The finished seam resembles a row of knit stitches.

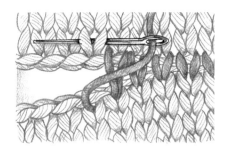

With the bound-off edges held together, lined up stitch for stitch, insert the yarn needle under a stitch inside the bound-off edge of one side and then under the corresponding stitch on the other side.

Invisible Vertical to Horizontal Seam on Stockinette Stitch

This seam is used to join bound-off stitches to rows, as in sewing the top of a sleeve to an armhole edge. Because there are usually more rows per inch (2.5cm) than stitches, occasionally pick up two horizontal bars on the piece with rows for a stitch on the bound-off piece.

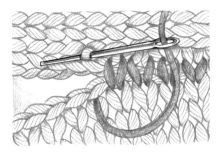

Insert the yarn needle under a stitch inside the bound-off edge of the vertical piece. Insert the needle under one or two horizontal bars between the first and second stitches of the horizontal piece.

PUTTING IN A ZIPPER

There are several types of zippers. Make sure to buy one that separates (the halves are not connected at all when unzipped) and has strong, durable metal or plastic teeth. You can purchase zippers in stores that sell sewing notions or online. Many online sources will make custom zippers to match your required length and color of tape with options for the heads and pulls.

MATERIALS
- Knitted pieces
- Zipper
- Pins
- Sewing needle
- Thread to match color of yarn

1) Place the knitted fabric on a flat surface with the right side facing.
2) Close the zipper and pin it in place, making sure the knitted fabric does not stretch or pucker. Take care that the zipper will not catch on the fabric when zipping or unzipping.
3) Baste the inner side of the zipper, and then backstitch along the zipper teeth. Remove the pins.

4) Turn the fabric to the wrong side and whip stitch the inner edge of the tape in place. Repeat for the opposite side, and remove the pins.

A zipper sewn into place on both fronts.

Troubleshooting
- If your zipper is a little too long, you can still use it. Align the bottom of the zipper with the bottom of the fabric, allowing the extra length to extend beyond the top of the knitted piece, and sew in place. Fold the excess length at the neck edge to the wrong side and whip stitch it in place.

- If you find that the fronts do not lay as flat as you like, you can always take it out and try again. Take your time on your next attempt, and make sure the fabric lays flat through the entire process.

SEWING IN A COLLAR

Four of the five adult replica cardigans require knitting a collar separately and then sewing it into place. You may do so by folding the collar in half with the wrong sides held together and then sewing through both thicknesses. If you find this to be difficult, you can use the method below.

1) Once the collar is complete, with right sides of both pieces facing, sew the bound-off edge of the collar along the neck opening.

2) Turn the cardigan so the wrong sides are facing, fold the collar in half width-wise to hide the WS of the collar, and carefully stitch the cast-on edge to the neck opening, enclosing the seam.

Use whichever method you find easiest and leaves you with the tidiest seam on the right side of the work.

Adding Buttons Instead of a Zipper

Mister Rogers' cardigans had zippers to make them easier to put on at the beginning of each episode. You, however, might prefer a buttoned cardigan. With some adjustments to the patterns in this book, you can include buttons instead of a zipper. These alterations require advance planning, a bit of design sense, and some careful math, so we recommend that only experienced knitters—or those up for a challenge—alter the patterns.

THINGS TO CONSIDER

Yarn quantities
Because you will add a button band and buttonhole band, you will need additional yarn. To be safe, buy an extra skein.

Button bands vs buttonhole bands
A button band is a piece of fabric to which buttons are sewn. A buttonhole band is worked in the same way except with buttonholes worked at intervals that align with the buttons on the button band. Choose on which side you will place each band. Traditionally, buttonhole bands are on the left front of men's garments and on the right front of women's garments.

Buttons
First, choose the size and style of button you'd like. Then determine how many buttons you'll need. You will want a button near the neck edge, another button near the hem edge, and then buttons spaced evenly along the front at 2–3"/ 5–7.5cm intervals.

Buttonholes
Buttonholes need to be the right size for your buttons. Knit a swatch with a buttonhole using the method found on the next page, or your own preferred method, and test it with your buttons. If the buttonhole is too small or large, adjust its size or choose different buttons that will work better.

Pattern for bands
Ribbed bands are common, but you can use any stitch pattern. Knit a gauge swatch in your chosen pattern, and use its gauge to determine how many stitches you need to either add or pick up. If you pick up stitches and your band pulls in then you have not picked up enough stitches. If your band flares out or ruffles then you have picked up too many stitches. In either case, rip out the band and adjust the number of stitches you pick up.

Width and Button/Buttonhole Placement
Button and buttonhole bands can be as wide as you want them to be, but we recommend making them approximately 1.5"/4cm wide. The bands will overlap when the cardigan is buttoned, so only the width of one band will be added to the combined width of the fronts. Work your buttonholes at the center of the width of the buttonhole band. Sew the buttons to the center of the width of the button band.

Collars
Four of the five replica cardigans require knitting a collar separately and then sewing it into place. For those cardigans, we suggest that you first work the bands and then sew in the collar (see page 123). Doing this allows you to align the collar to the center or either edge of the bands, according to your preference.

RECOMMENDED METHODS

Button and buttonhole bands can be added to garments in a variety of ways. For the cardigans in this book, we recommend following the method below for each. Below you will find general instructions that you must adapt to your stitch pattern, button spacing, and so forth. Don't forget to add the buttonholes on your preferred side.

Picked up
- Friendly Neighbor Cardigan (pages 10–13)
- Beginnings Cardigan (pages 14–17)

Measure the length of your front from cast-on edge to the beginning of the collar shaping. Use this measurement and the gauge from the swatch you made for the bands to calculate how many stitches you need to pick up and knit along the fronts. Pick up the appropriate number of stitches, keeping in mind the pattern stitch repeat, and work the bands.

Knitted-In Vertically
- Generosity Cardigan (pages 18–21)

Work the pattern as written, but place your buttonholes in the front band on your preferred side. Because these bands will be included in the original measurements, when buttoned, the front will be approximately 1.5"/4cm narrower than the back and the black piping will no longer be centered.

Knitted-In horizontally
- Nurture Cardigan (pages 22–25)
- Beautiful Day Cardigan (pages 26–29)

When working each front, cast on 6 extra stitches. Work those extra stitches into the rib stated in the pattern, placing the buttonholes 2 or 3 stitches in from the edge. When you reach the neck shaping, bind off those extra stitches in addition to the stated number of stitches in the pattern and continue as written.

BUTTONHOLES

There are many different ways to work a buttonhole, but we will include a simple and easy version. This version calls for a buttonhole that will be 4 stitches wide. If you find that this creates buttonholes that are too narrow or too wide for your buttons, you can adjust the number of stitches you bind off on the first row and then cast on the following row. If adjusting the width, remember to consider the new width when you determine buttonhole placement on the buttonhole band to keep them centered.

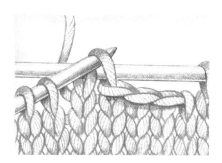

Row 1 Work to placement of buttonhole: k2, lift 2nd st on RH needle over first st and off needle, [k1, lift 2nd st over first st] 3 times, work to end—4 sts have been bound off.

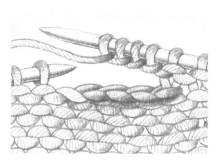

Row 2 Work to bound-off sts, cast on 4 sts using backwards loop cast-on.

Row 3 Work cast-on sts in pat tbl to tighten.

A completed buttonhole worked in a background of Stockinette stitch.

Techniques

3-NEEDLE BIND-OFF

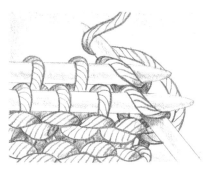

1) Hold right sides of pieces together on two needles. Insert third needle knitwise into first stitch of each needle, and wrap yarn knitwise.

2) Knit these two stitches together, and slip them off the needles. *Knit the next two stitches together in the same manner.

3) Slip first stitch on third needle over second stitch and off needle. Rep from * in step 2 across row until all stitches are bound off.

KITCHENER STITCH

Cut a tail at least 4 times the length of the edge that will be grafted together and thread through a tapestry needle. Hold needles together with right sides showing, making sure each has the same number of live stitches, and work as follows:

1) Insert tapestry needle purlwise through first stitch on front needle. Pull yarn through, leaving stitch on needle.

2) Insert tapestry needle knitwise through first stitch on back needle. Pull yarn through, leaving stitch on needle.

3) Insert tapestry needle knitwise through first stitch on front needle, pull yarn through, and slip stitch off needle. Then, insert tapestry needle purlwise through next stitch on front needle and pull yarn through, leaving this stitch on needle.

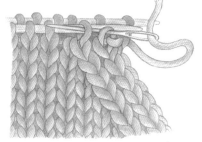

4) Insert tapestry needle purlwise through first stitch on back needle, pull yarn through, and slip stitch off needle. Then, insert tapestry needle knitwise through next stitch on back needle and pull yarn through, leaving this stitch on needle.

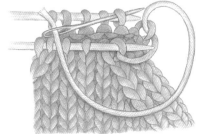

Repeat steps 3 and 4 until all stitches on both front and back needles have been grafted.

EMBROIDERY STITCHES

Chain Stitch

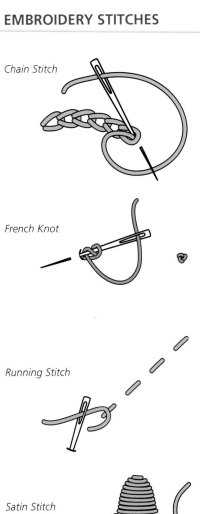

French Knot

Running Stitch

Satin Stitch

Straight Stitch

Whip Stitch

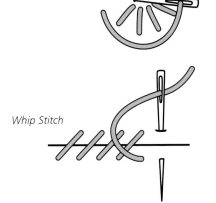

SHORT-ROW WRAP AND TURN (W&T)

When short rows are needed for shaping, some patterns ask you to wrap your stitches to prevent holes in the work.
Wrapping a stitch on the right side is a little different than when on the wrong side, but they are basically the same.

Knit Side

1) With the yarn in back, slip the next stitch purlwise.

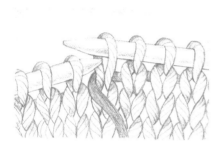

2) Move the yarn between the needles to the front of the work.

3) Slip the same stitch back to the left needle. Turn the work, bringing the yarn to the purl side between the needles. One stitch is wrapped.

4) When you have completed all the short rows, you must hide the wraps. Work to just before the wrapped stitch. Insert the right needle under the wrap and knitwise into the wrapped stitch. Knit them together.

Purl Side

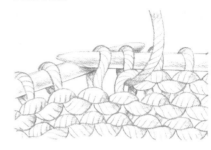

1) With the yarn at the front, slip the next stitch purlwise.

2) Move the yarn between the needles to the back of the work.

3) Slip the same stitch back to the left needle. Turn the work, bringing the yarn back to the purl side between the needles. One stitch is wrapped.

4) After working the short rows, you must hide the wraps. Work to just before the wrapped stitch. Insert the right needle from behind into the back loop of the wrap and place it on the left needle as shown. Purl it together with the stitch on the left needle.

Index